This Book Belongs To

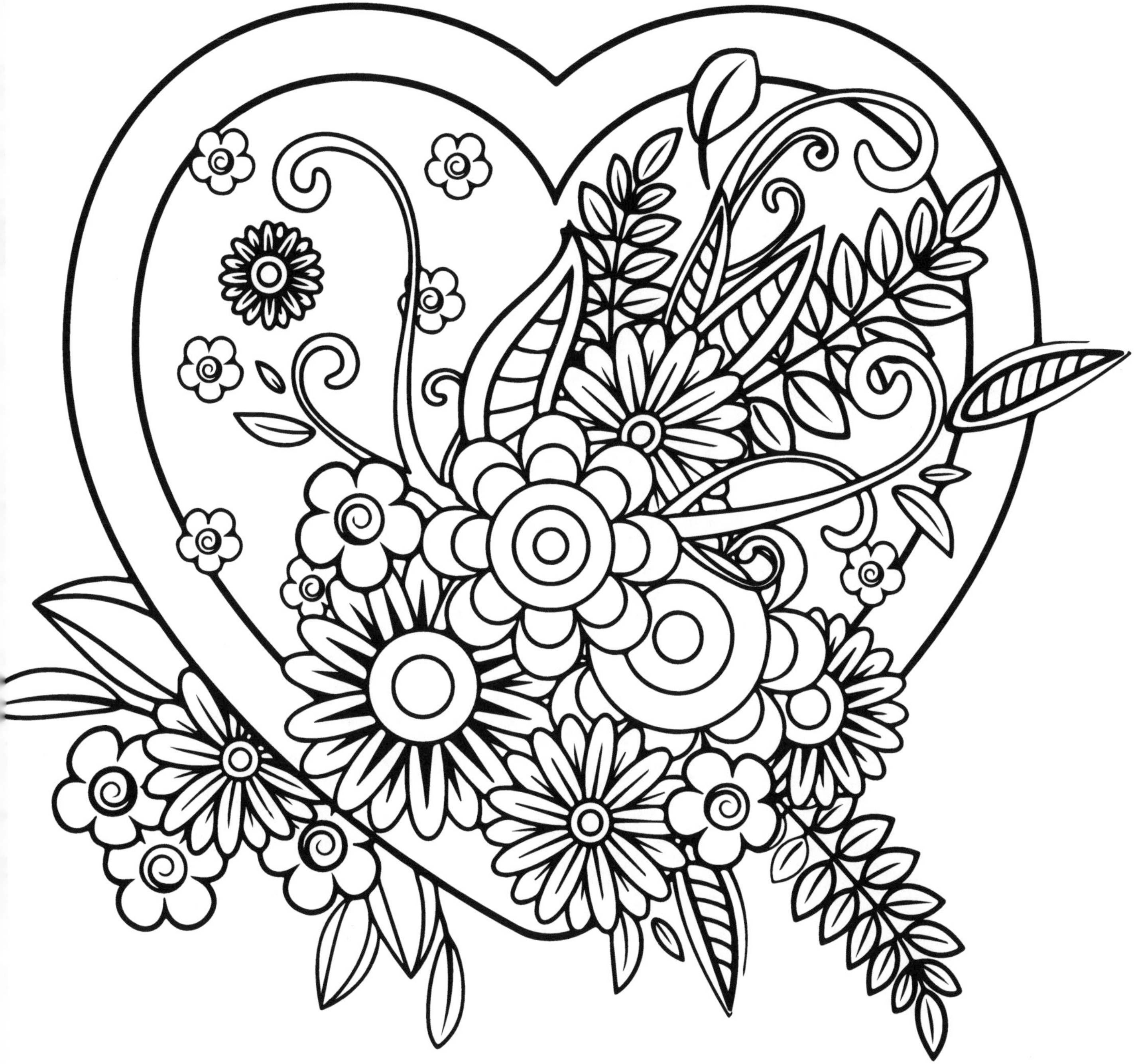

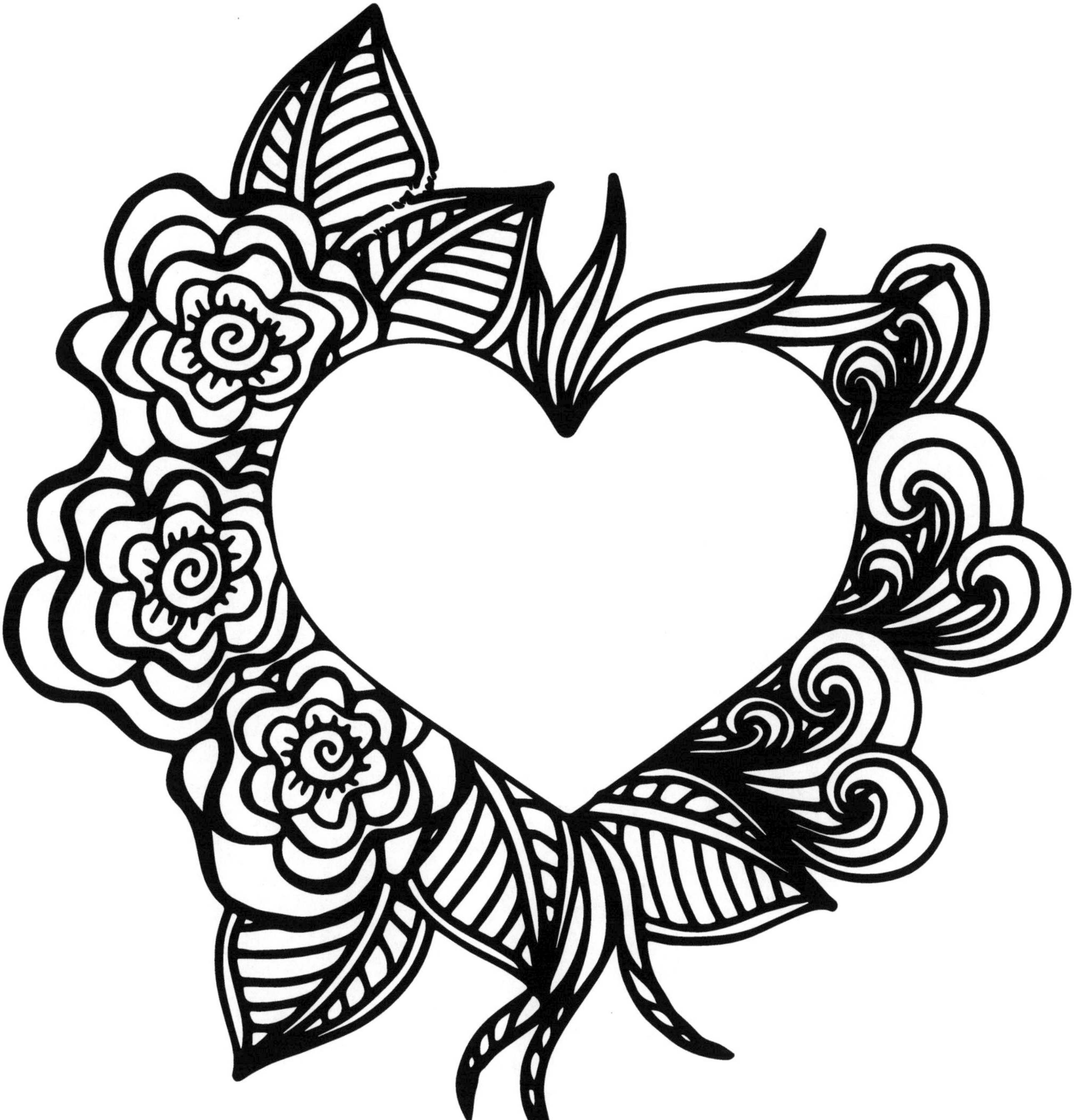

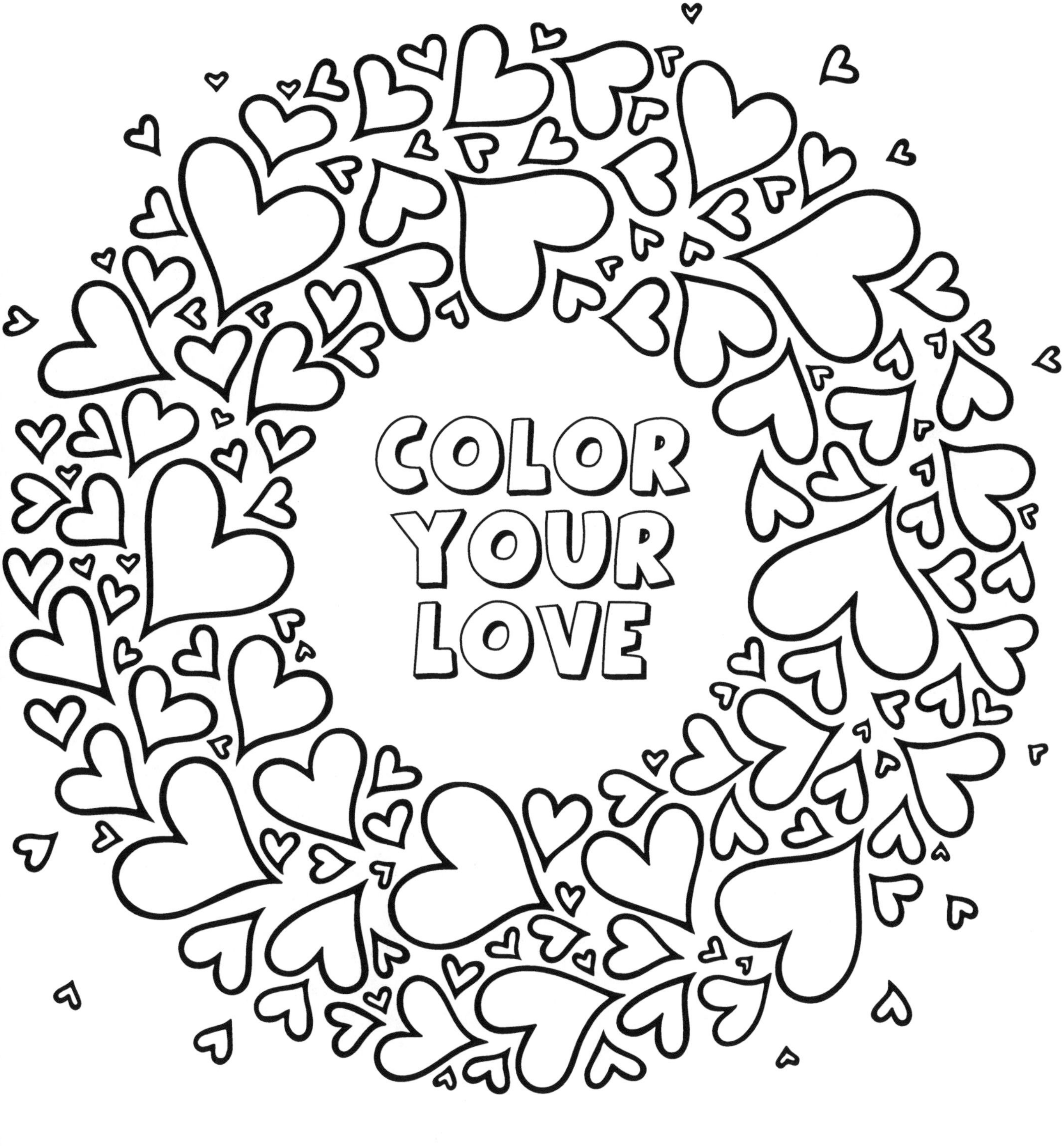
COLOR
YOUR
LOVE

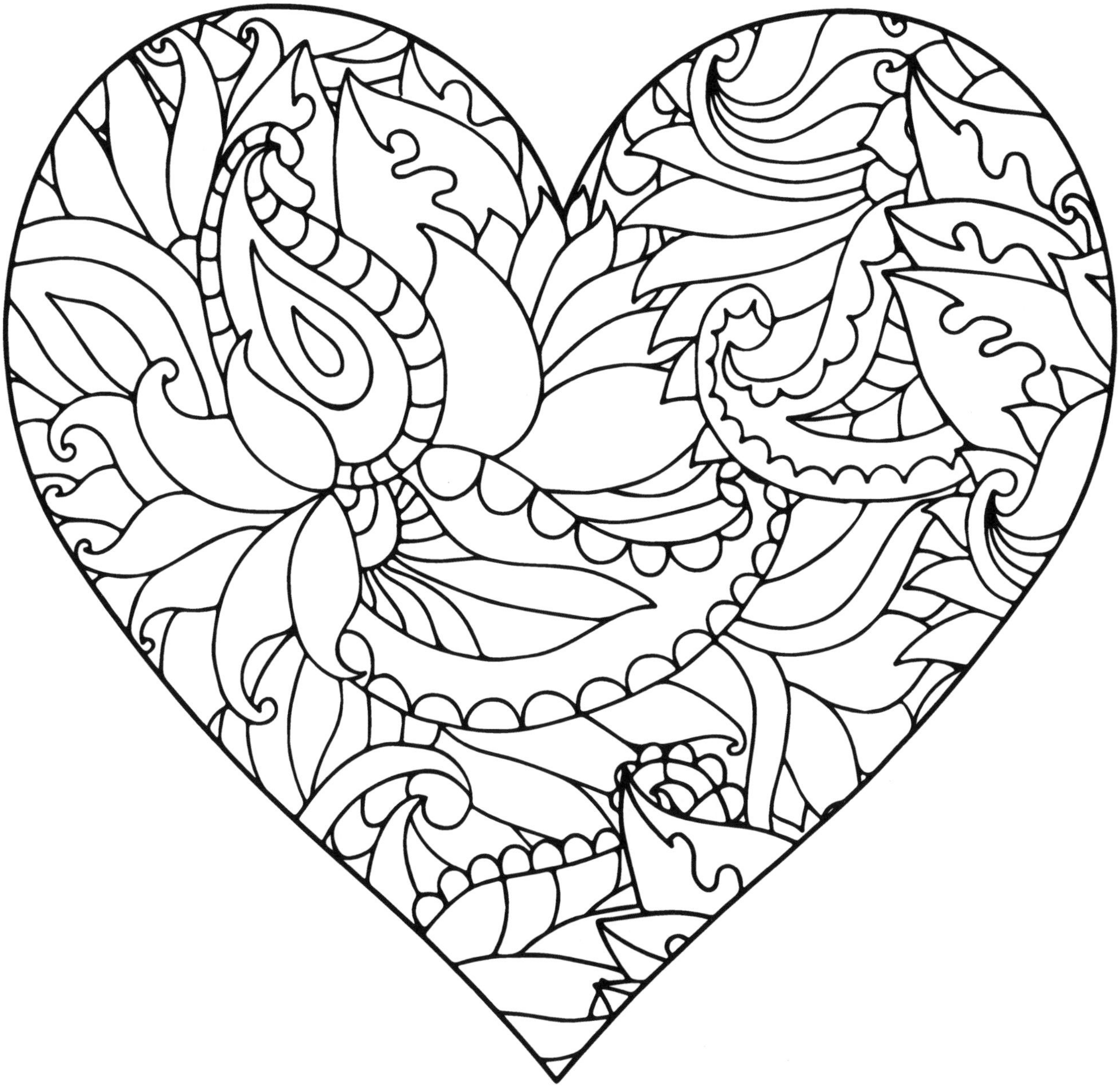

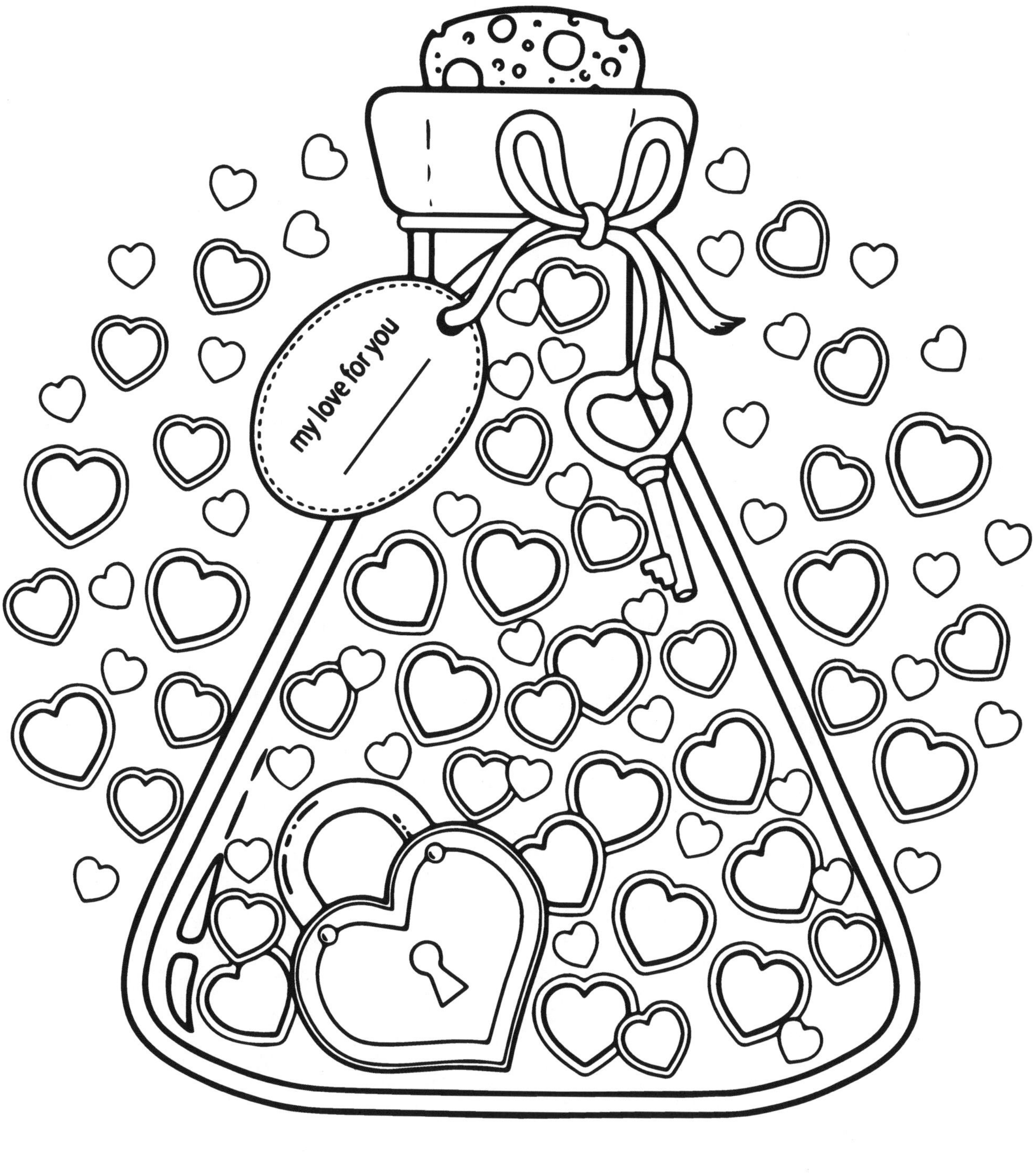
my love for you

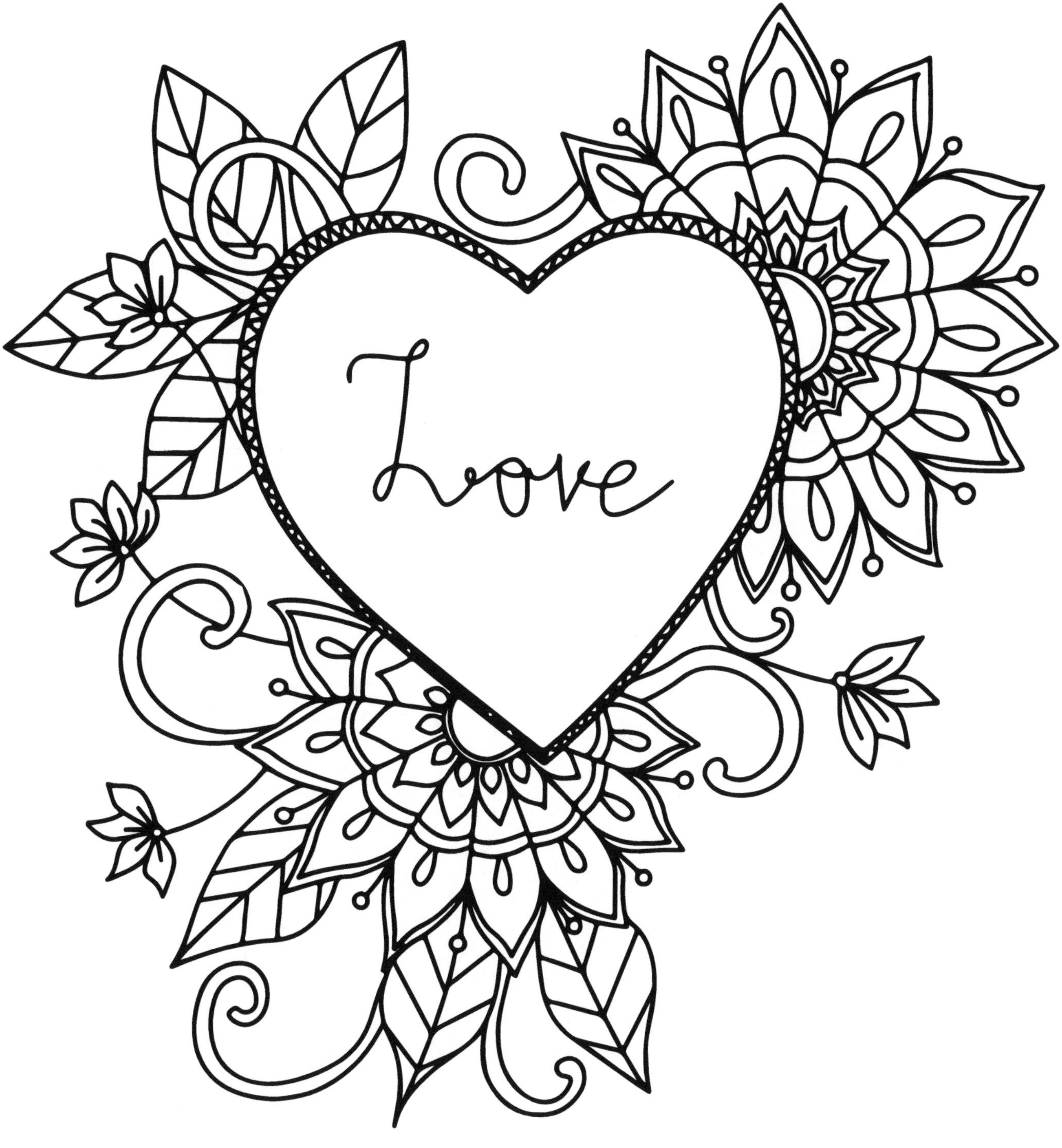
Love

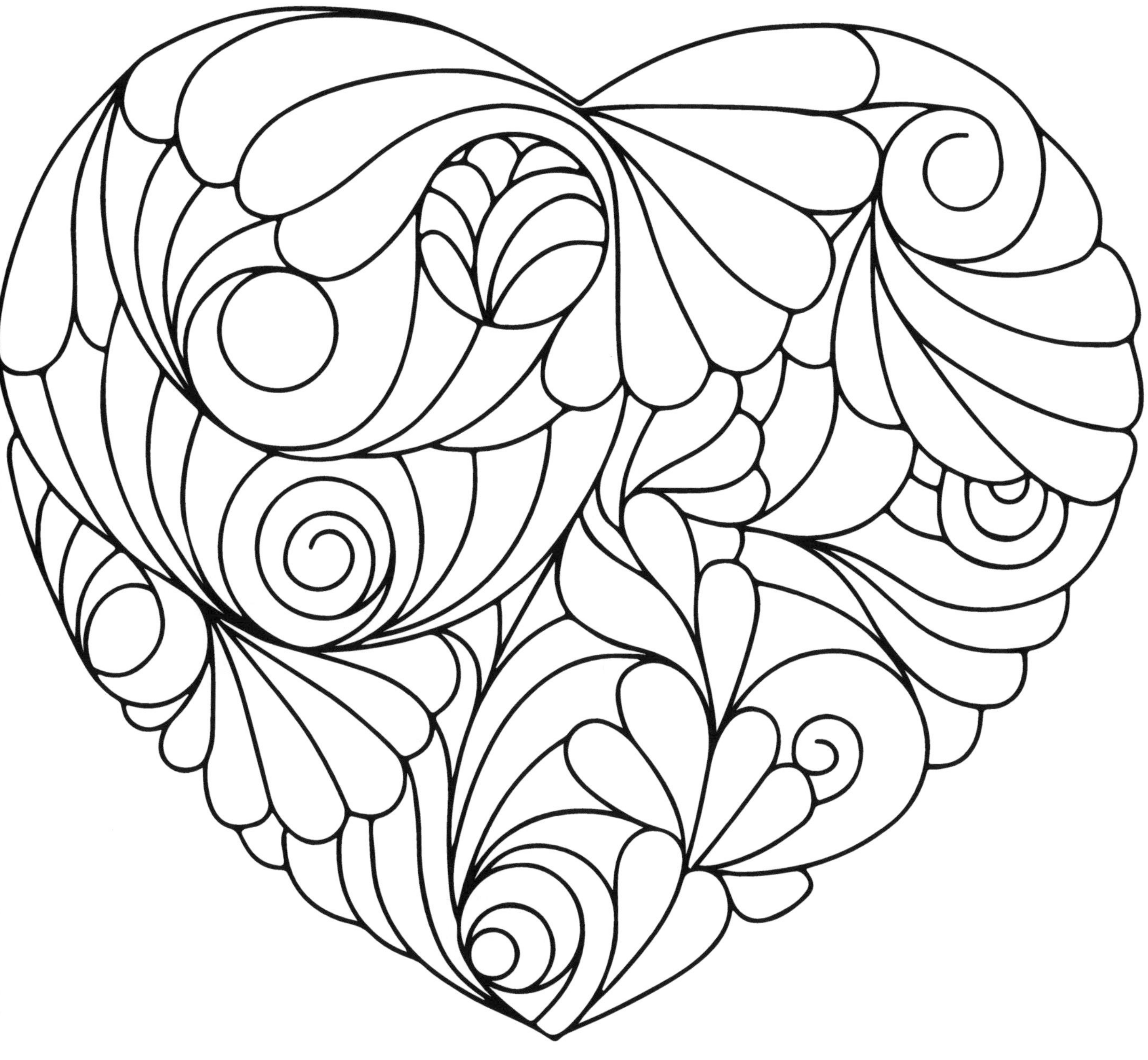

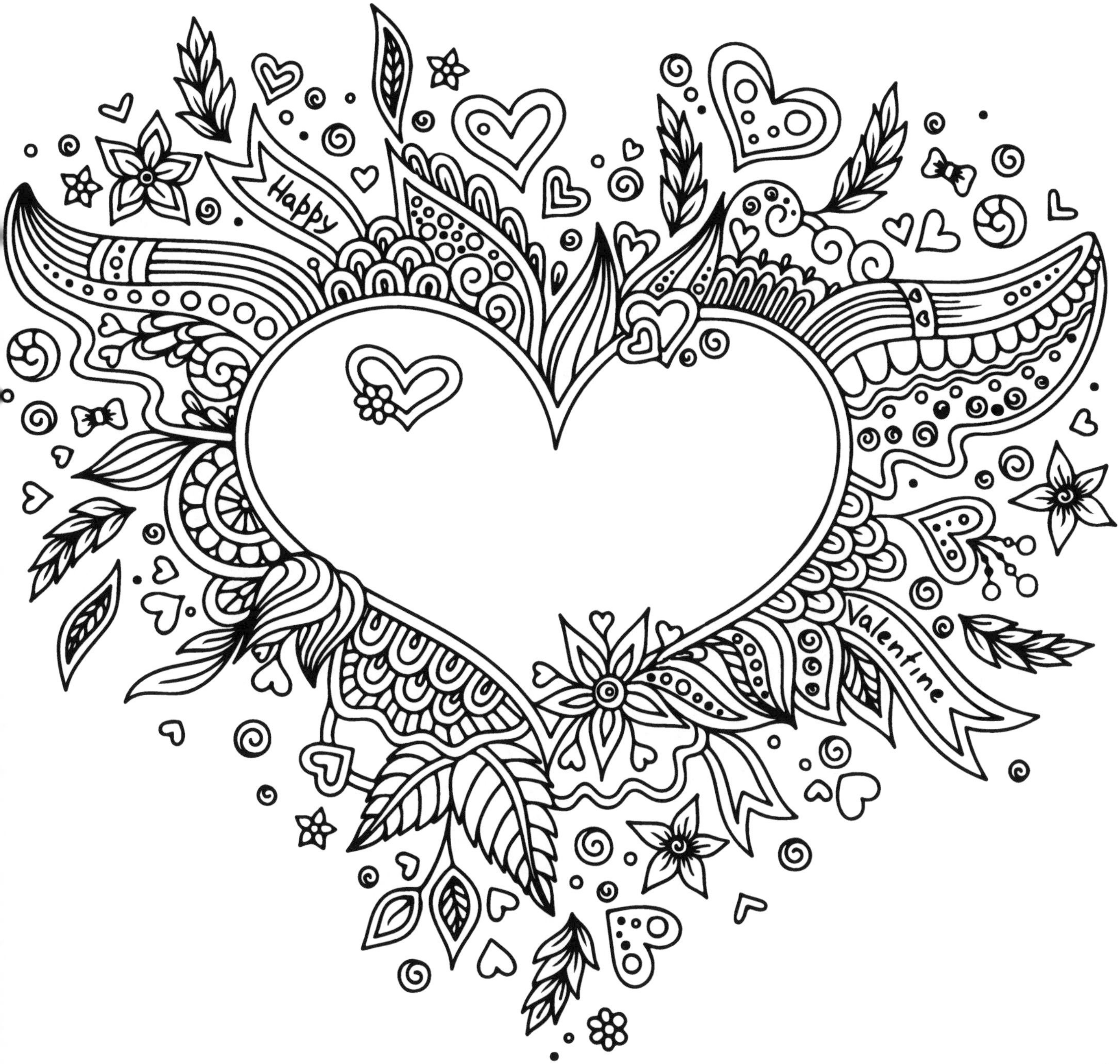
Happy
Valentine

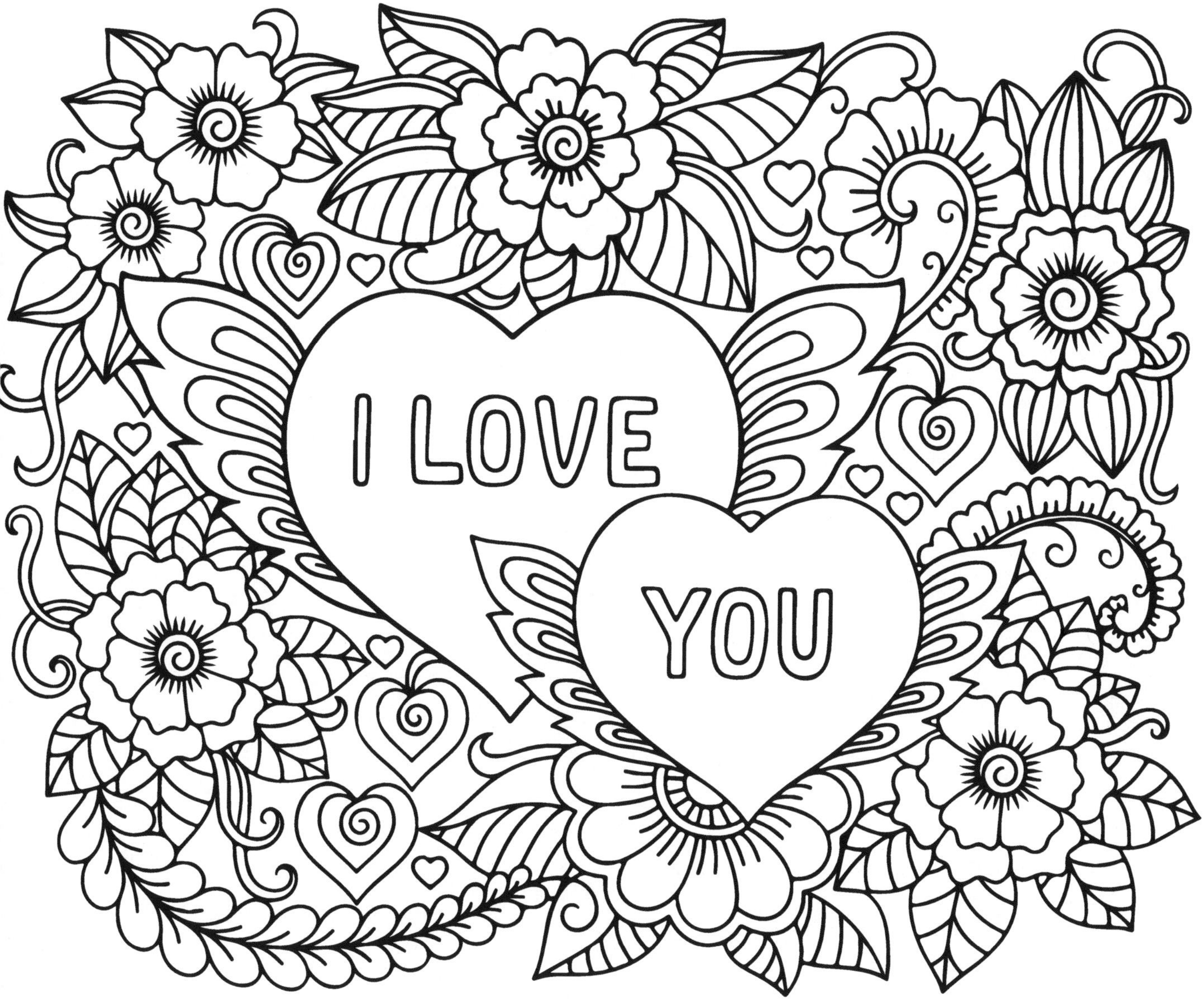
I LOVE
YOU

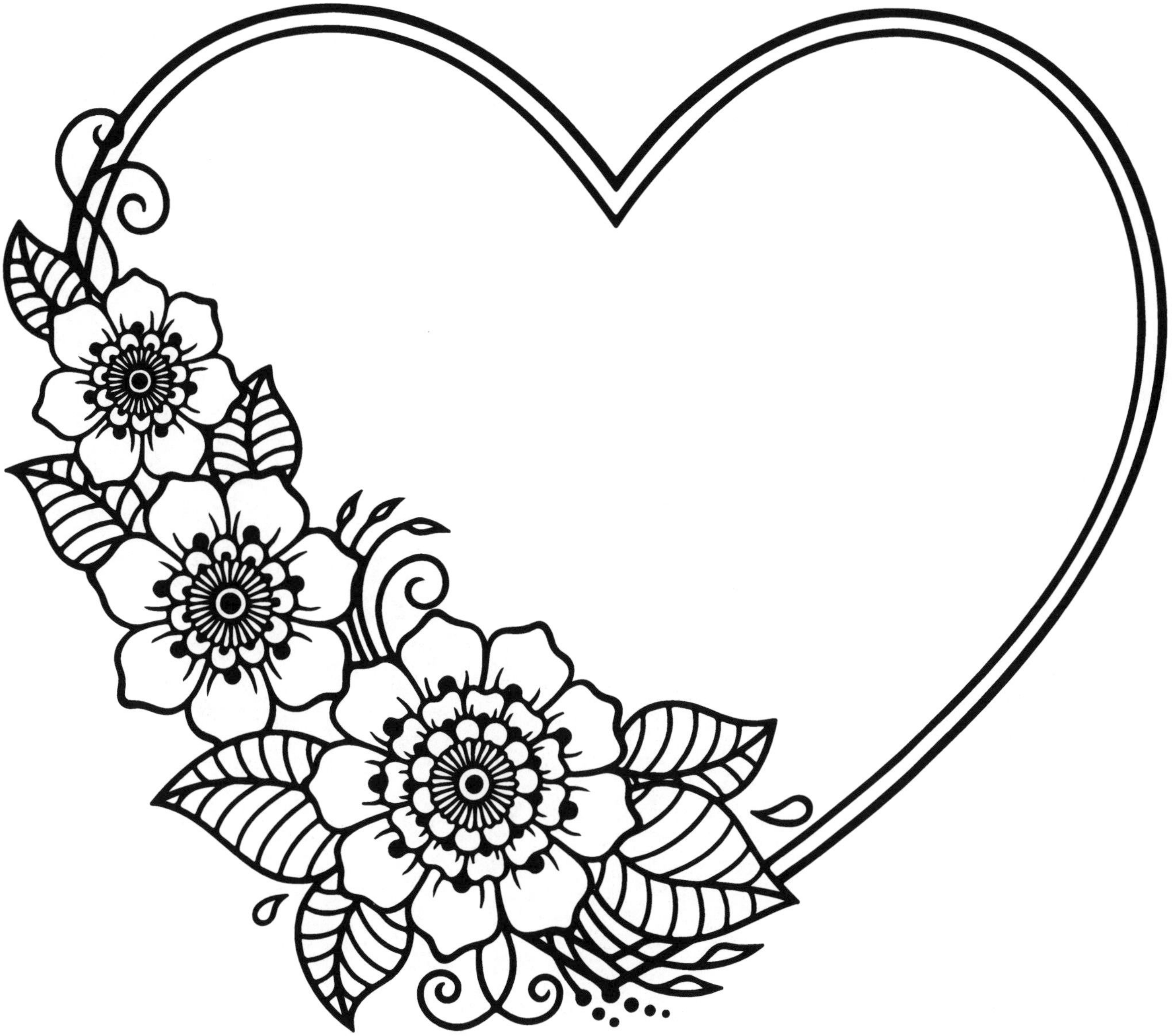

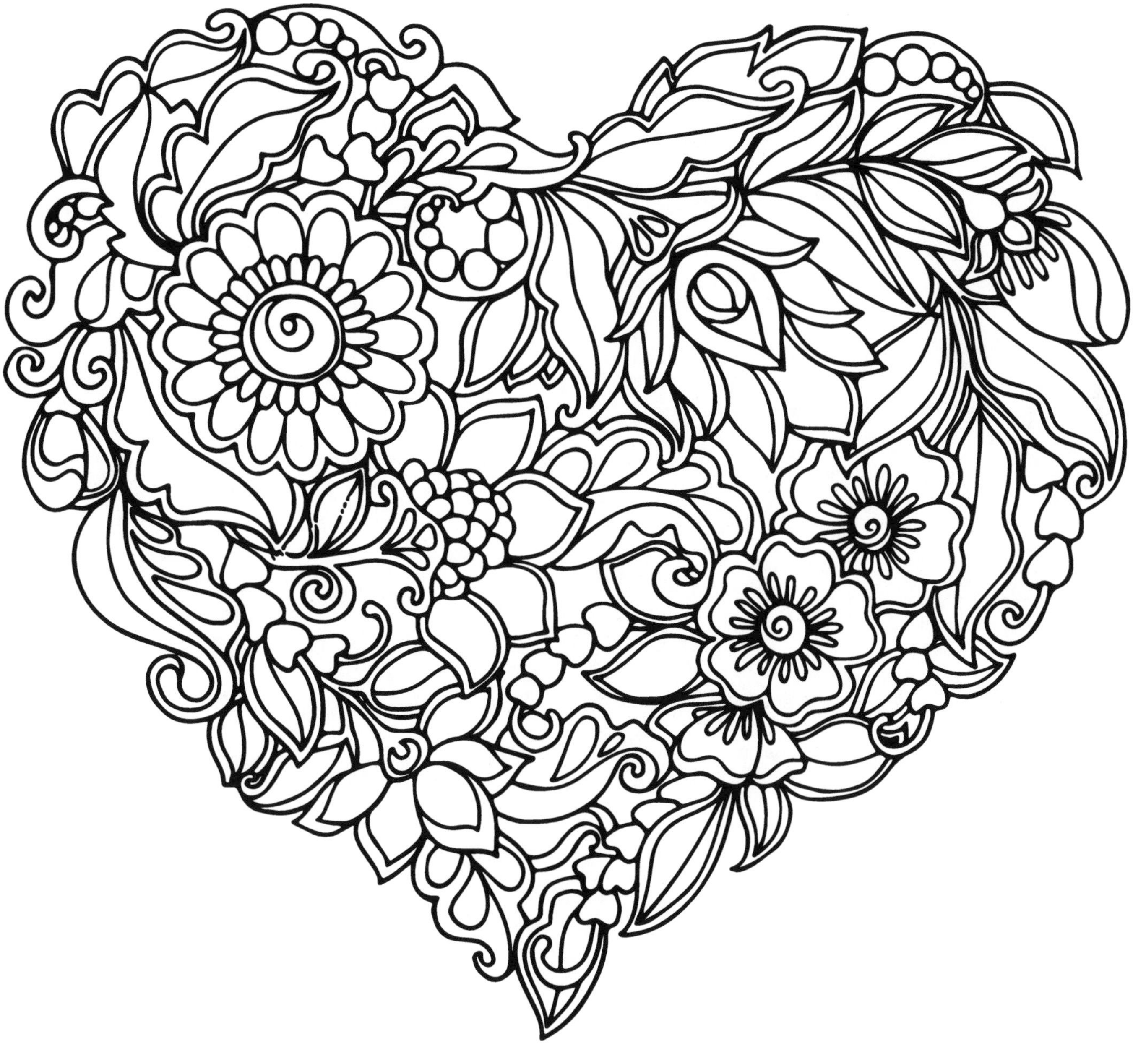

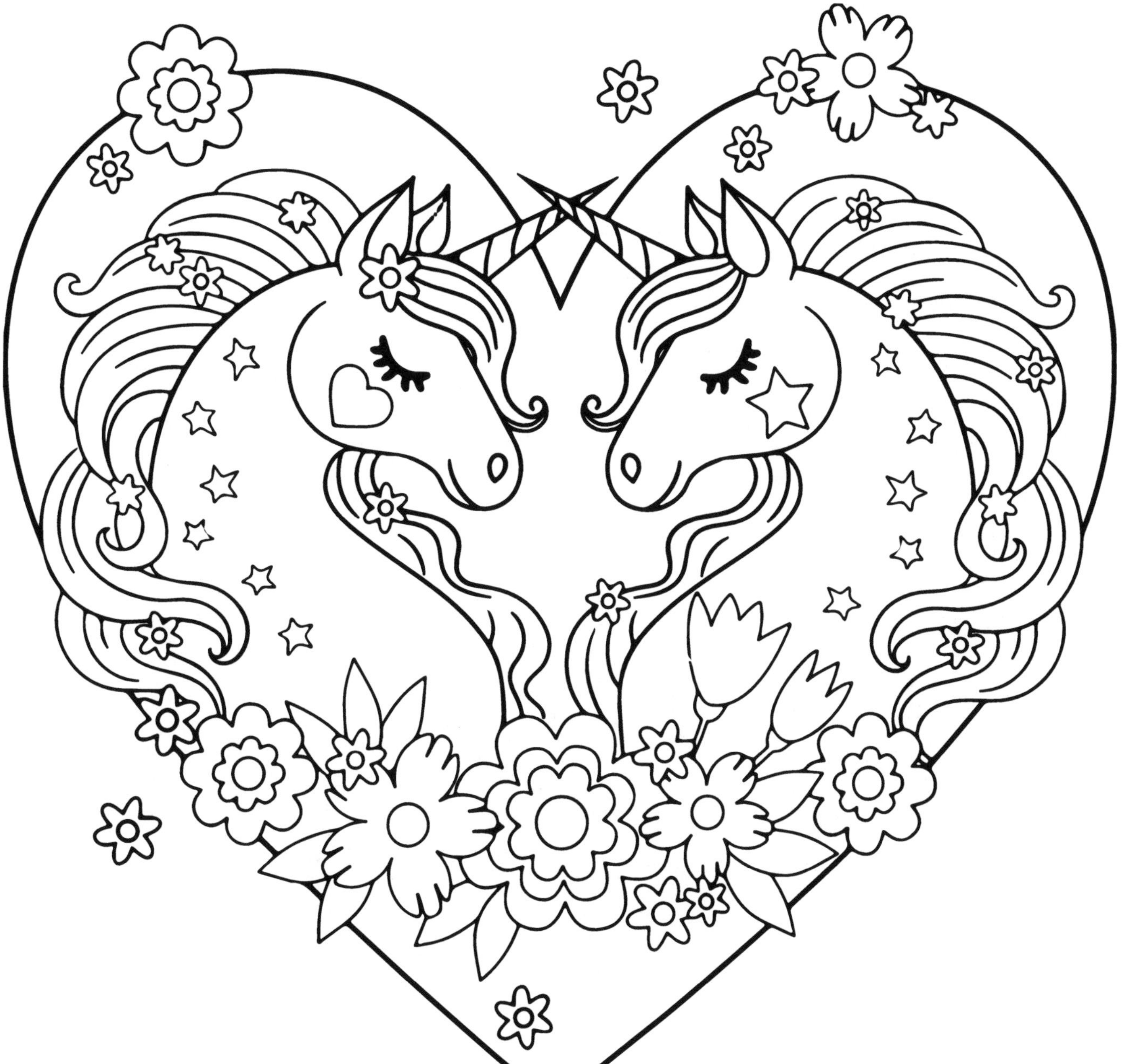

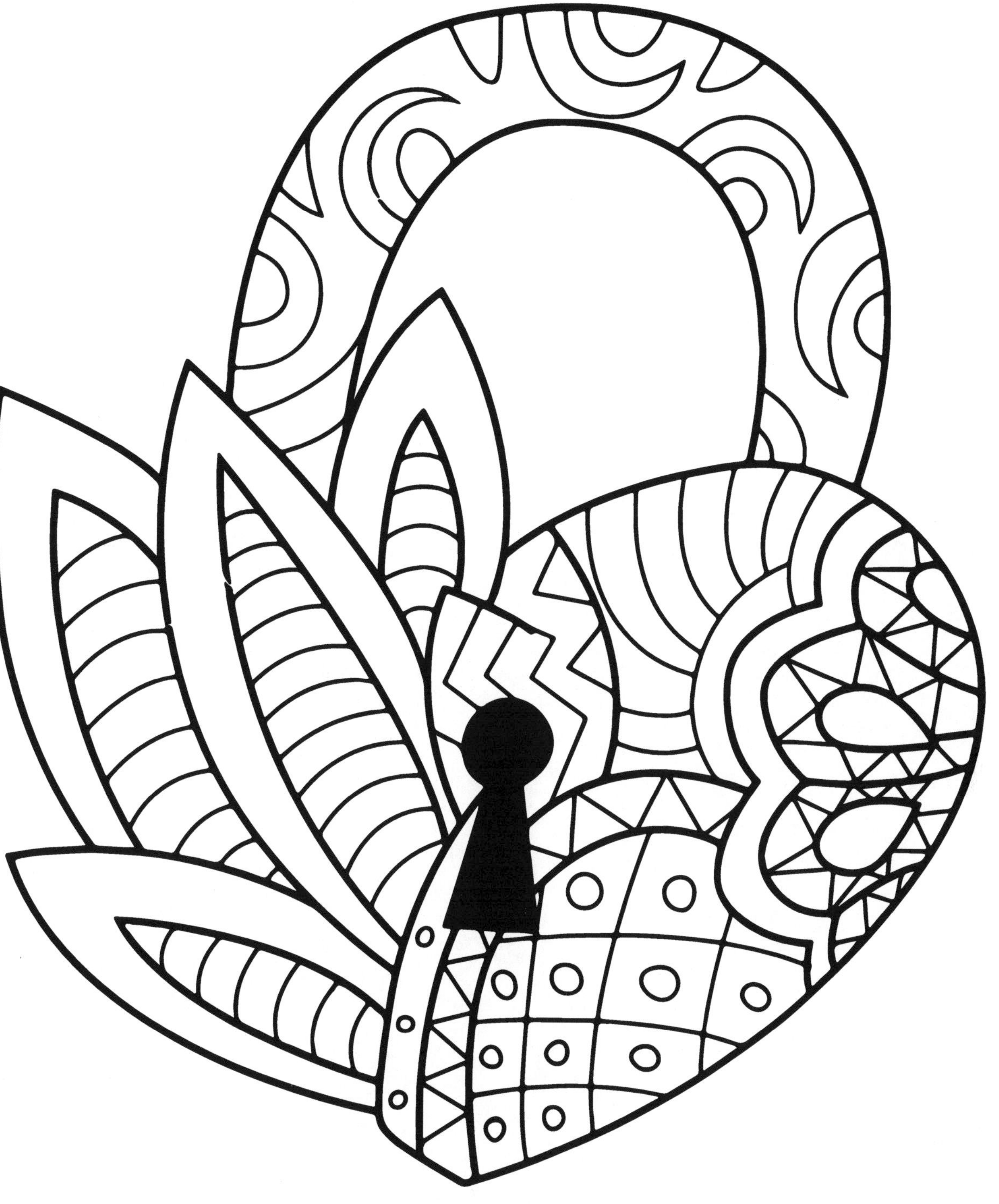

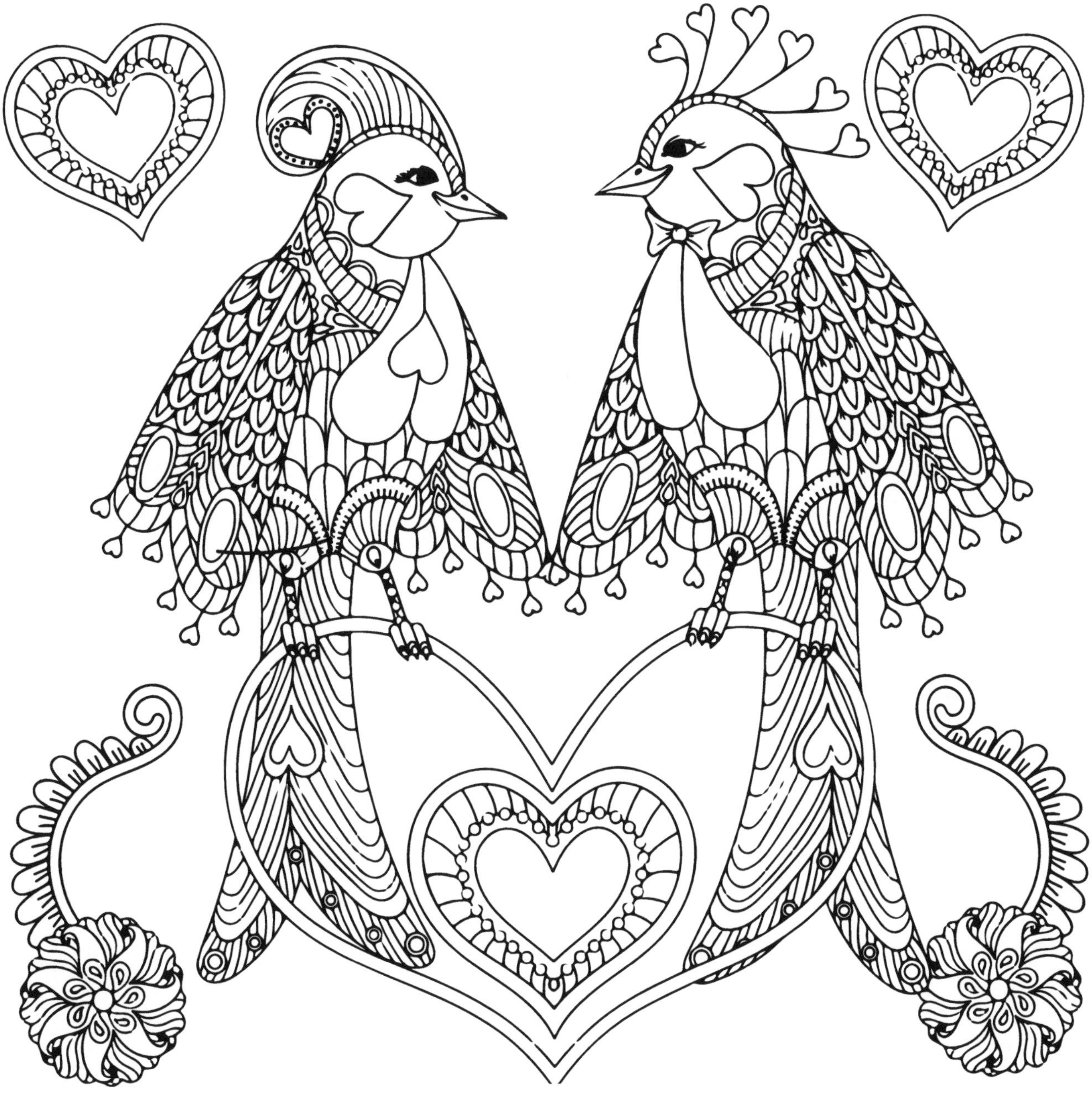

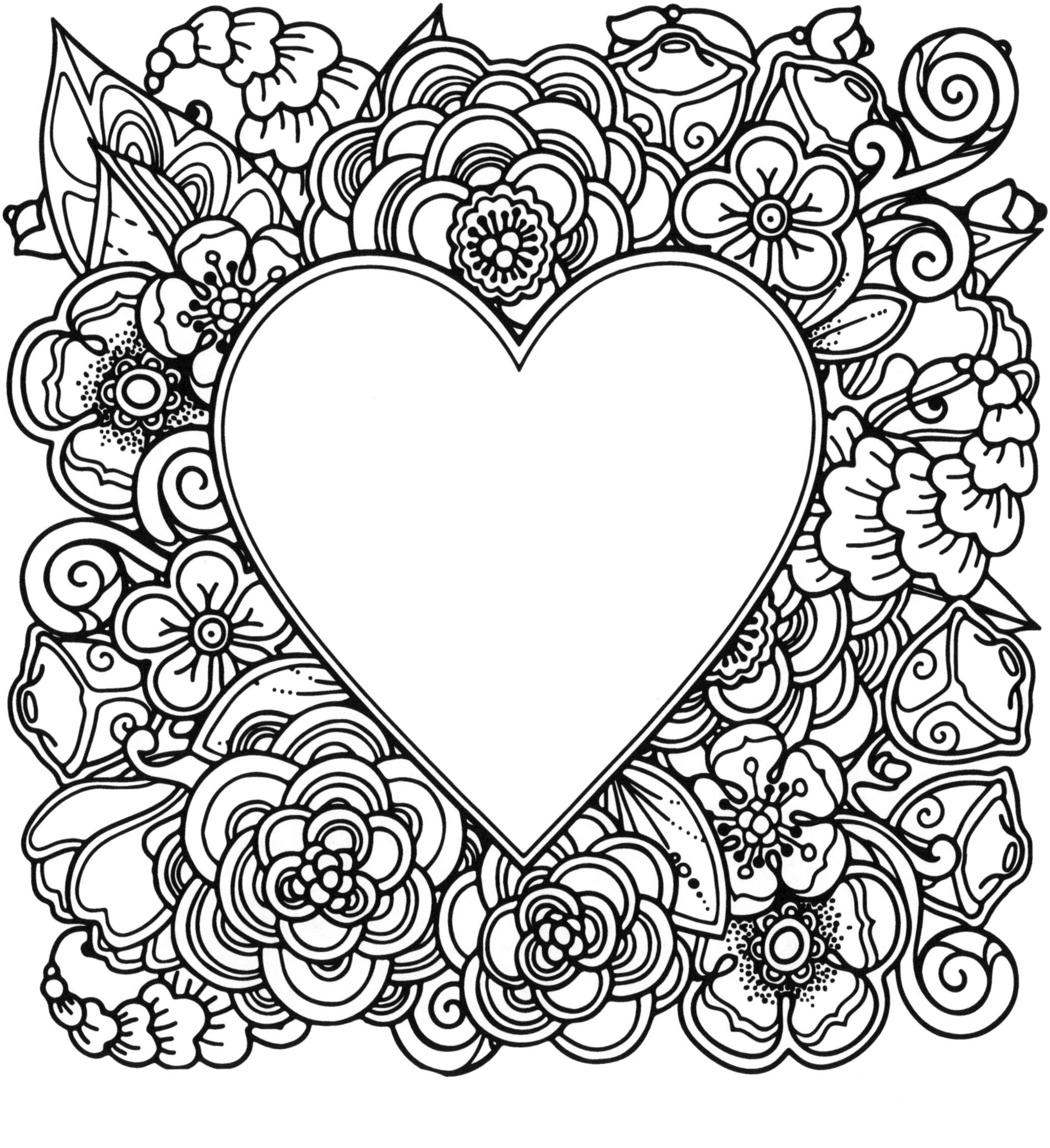

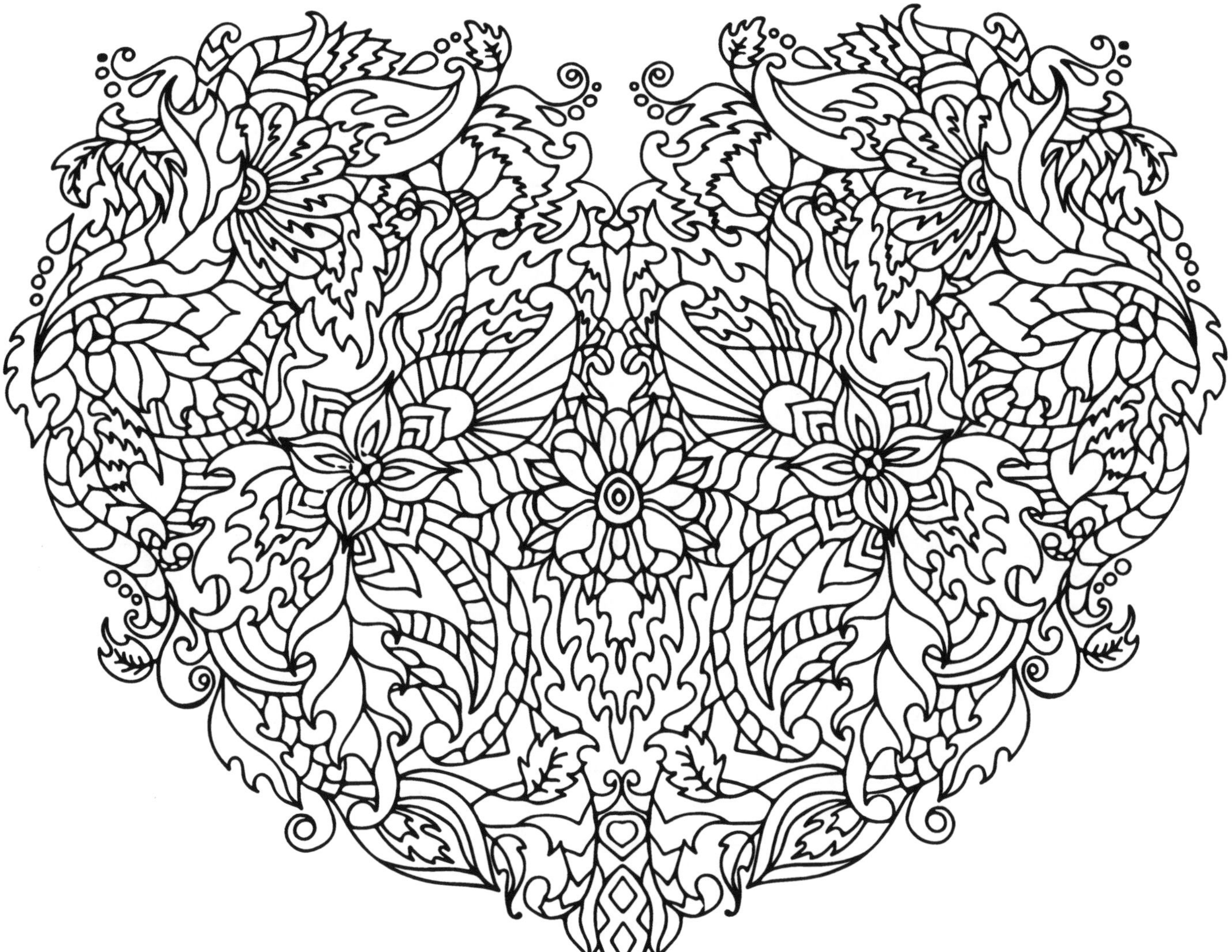

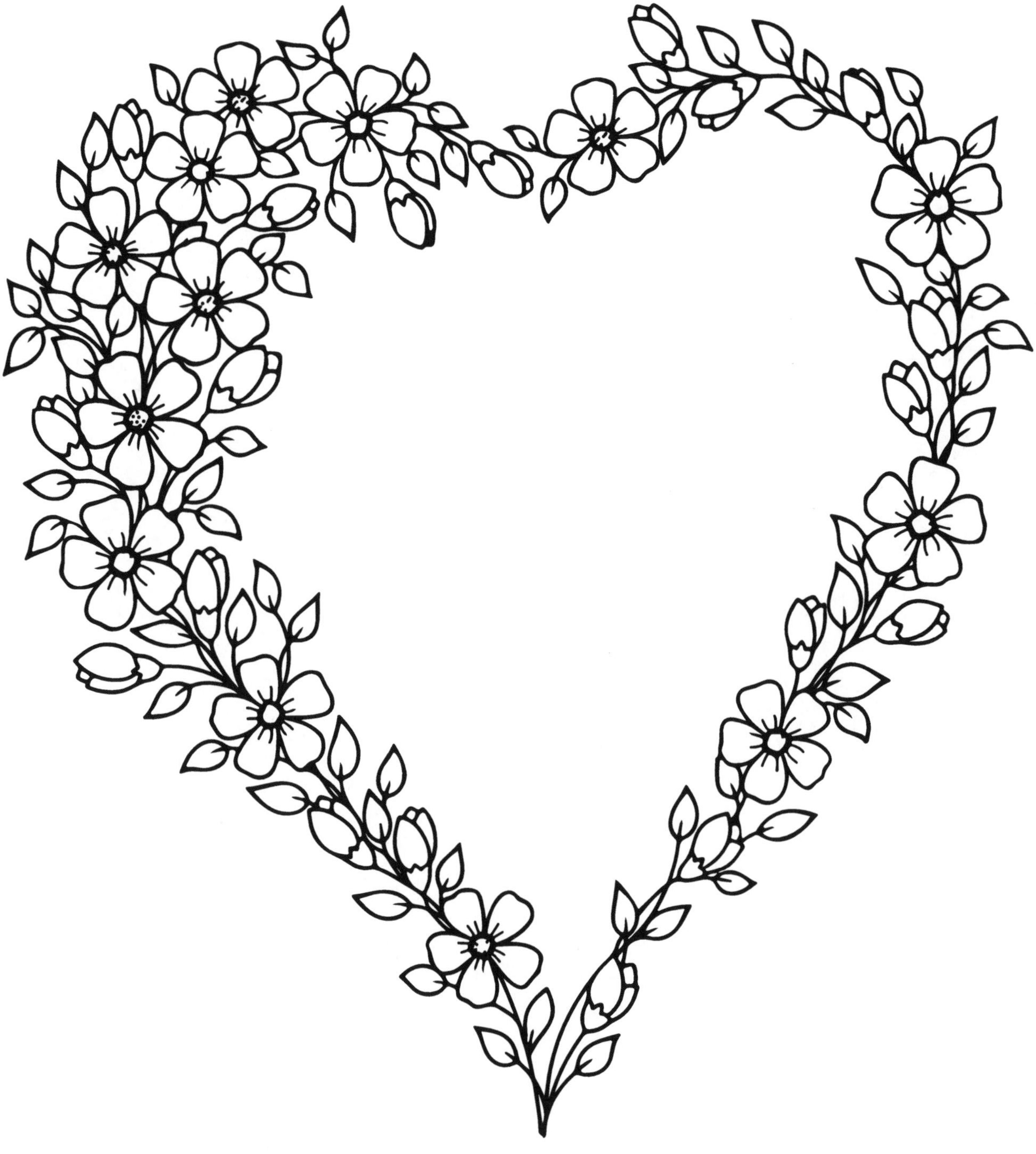

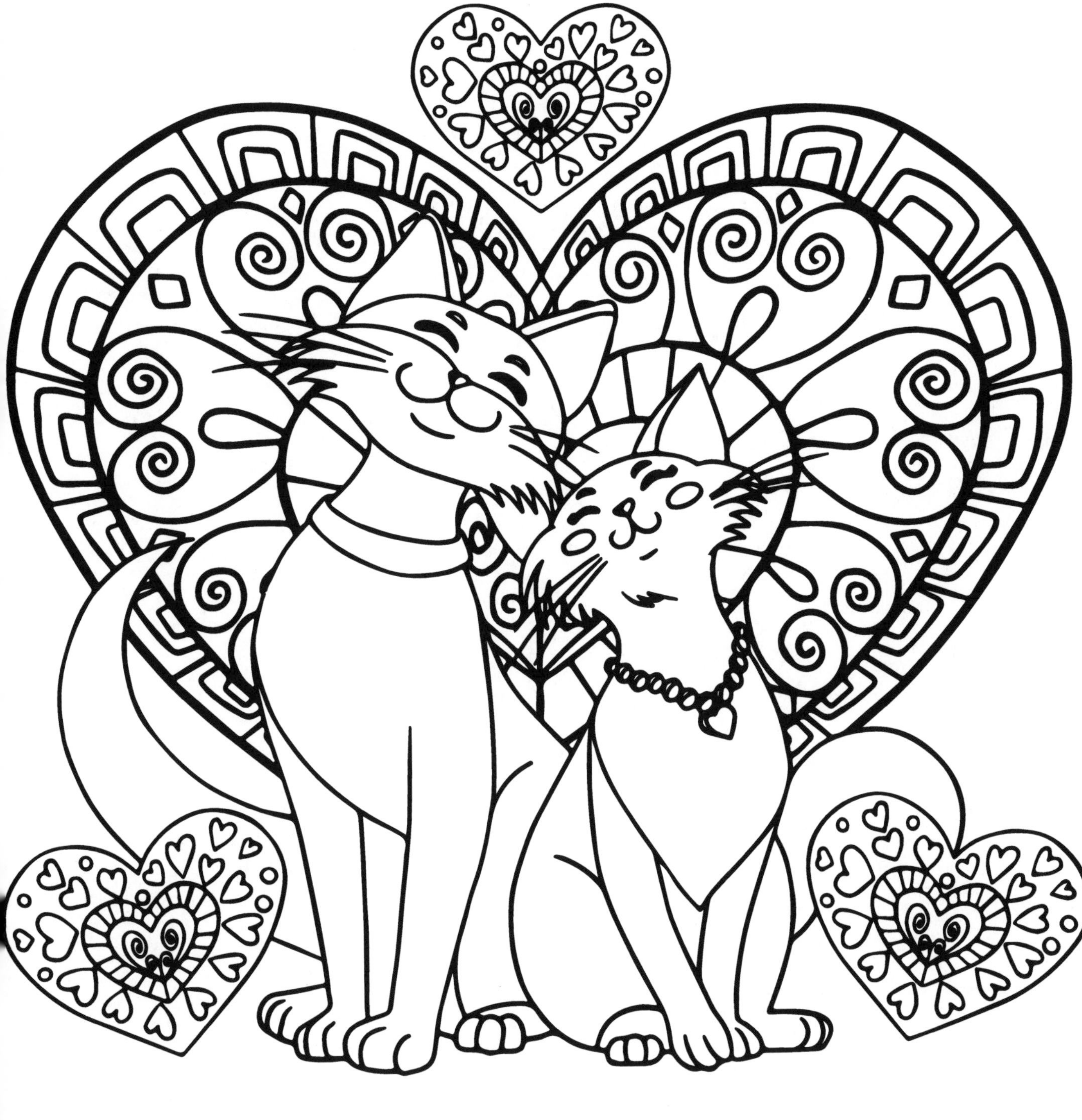

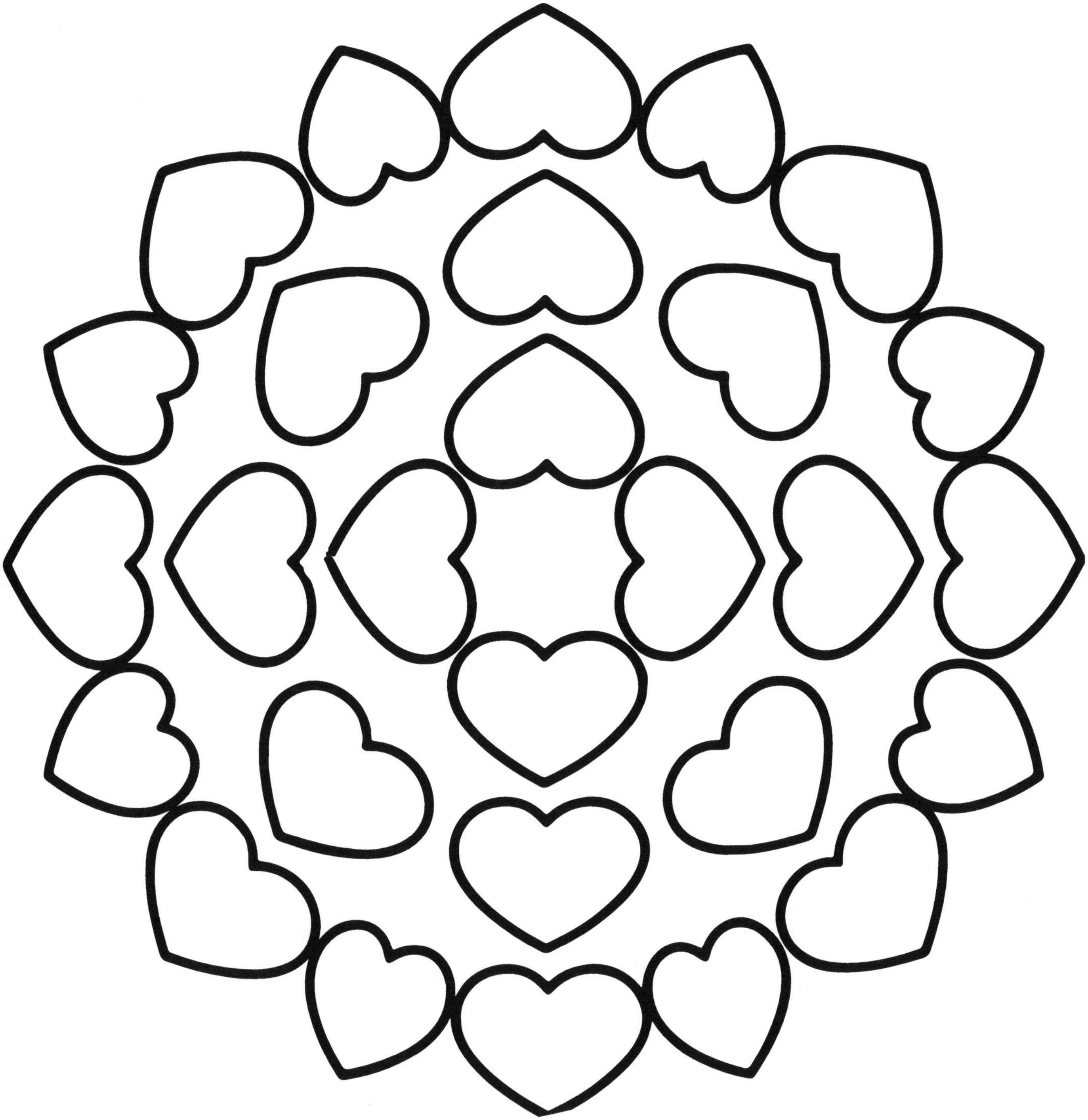

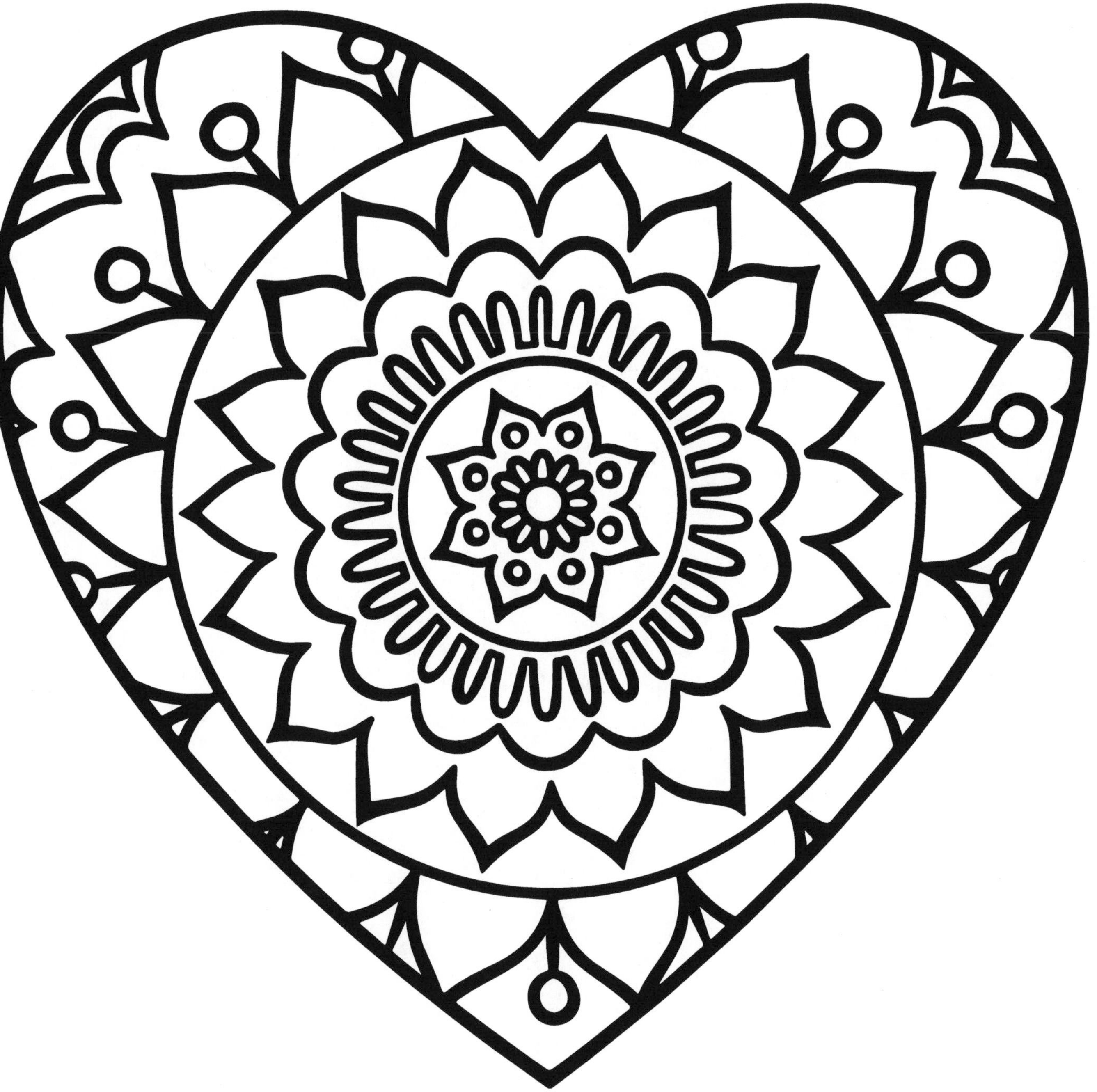

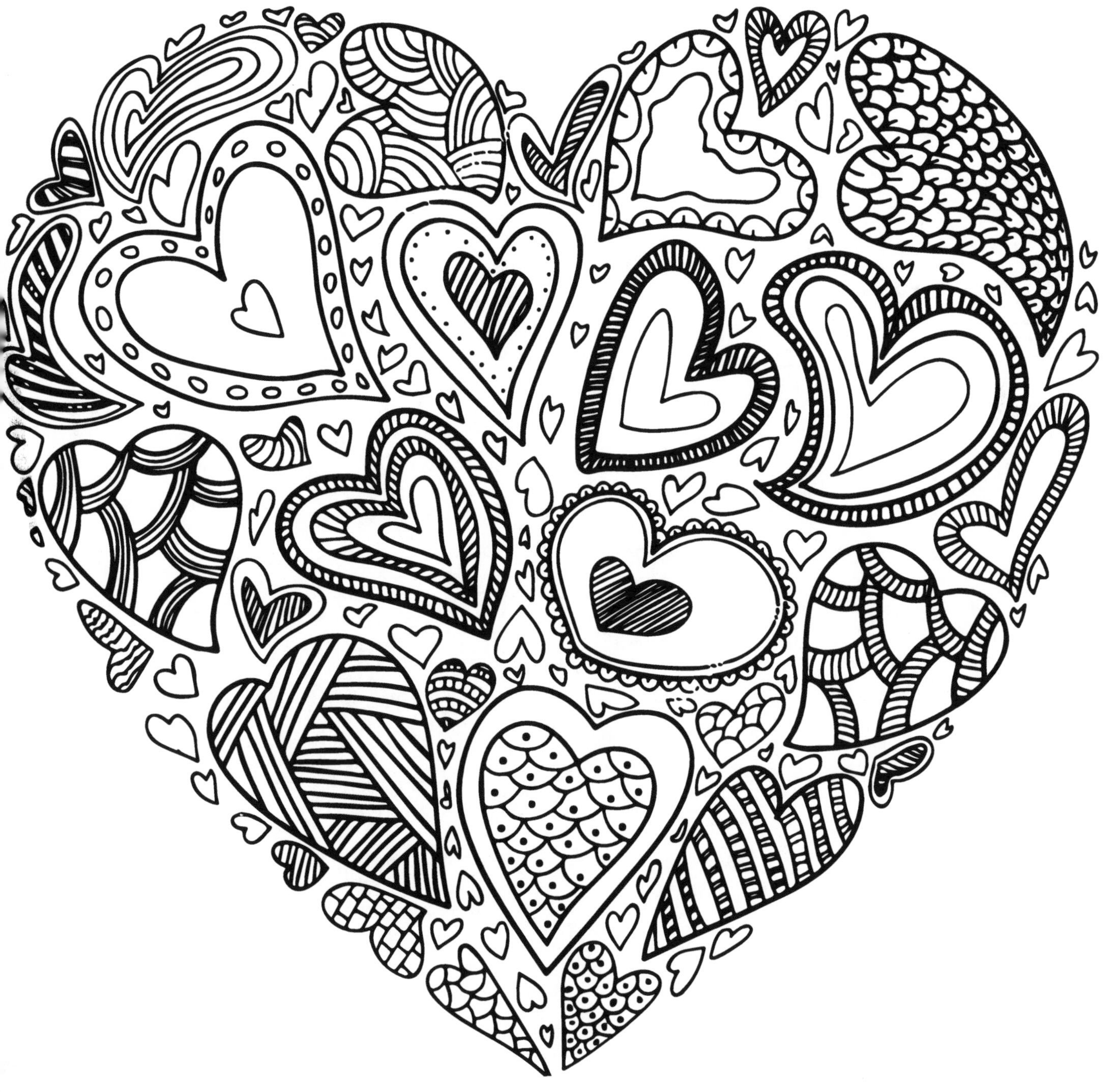

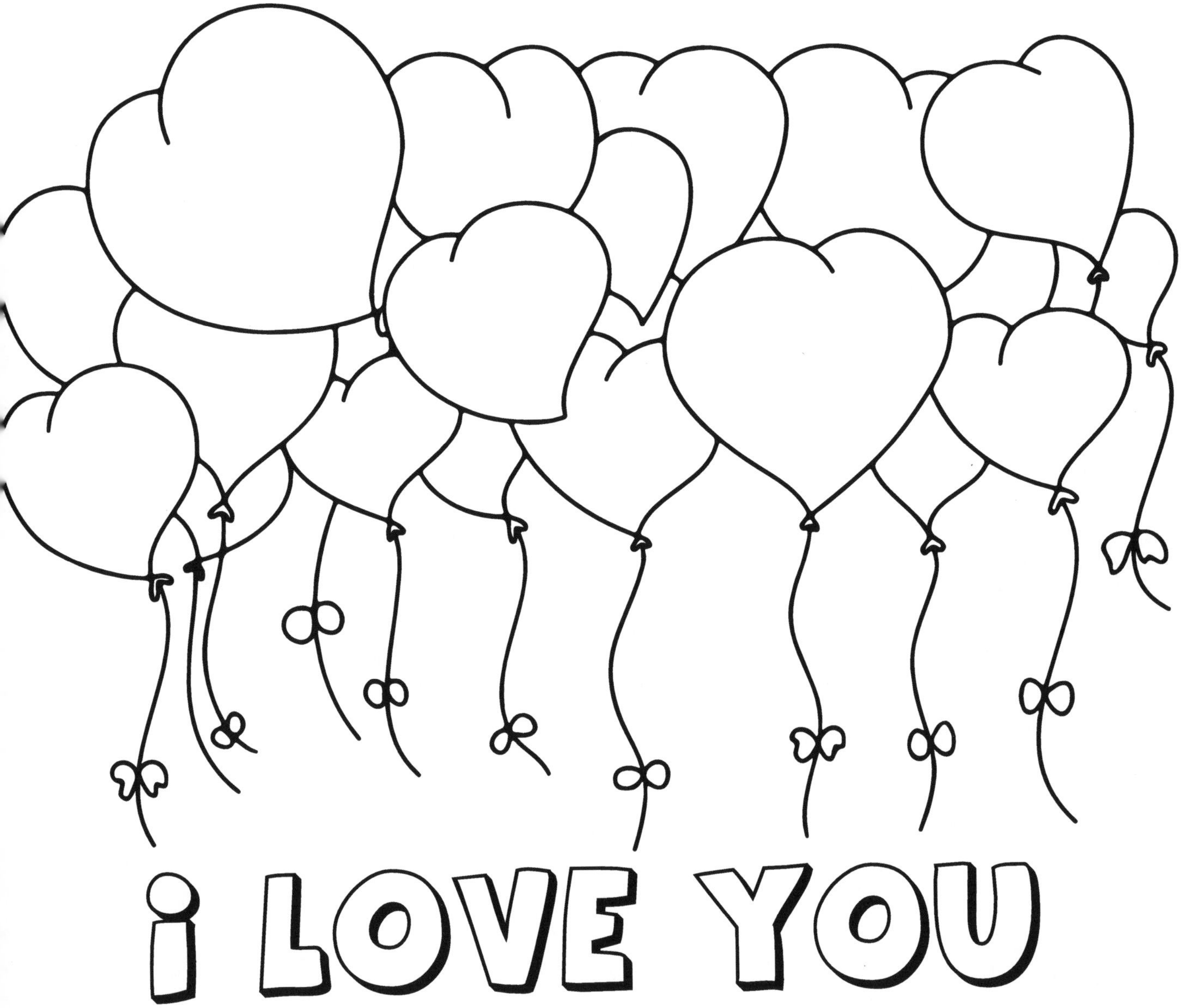

I LOVE YOU

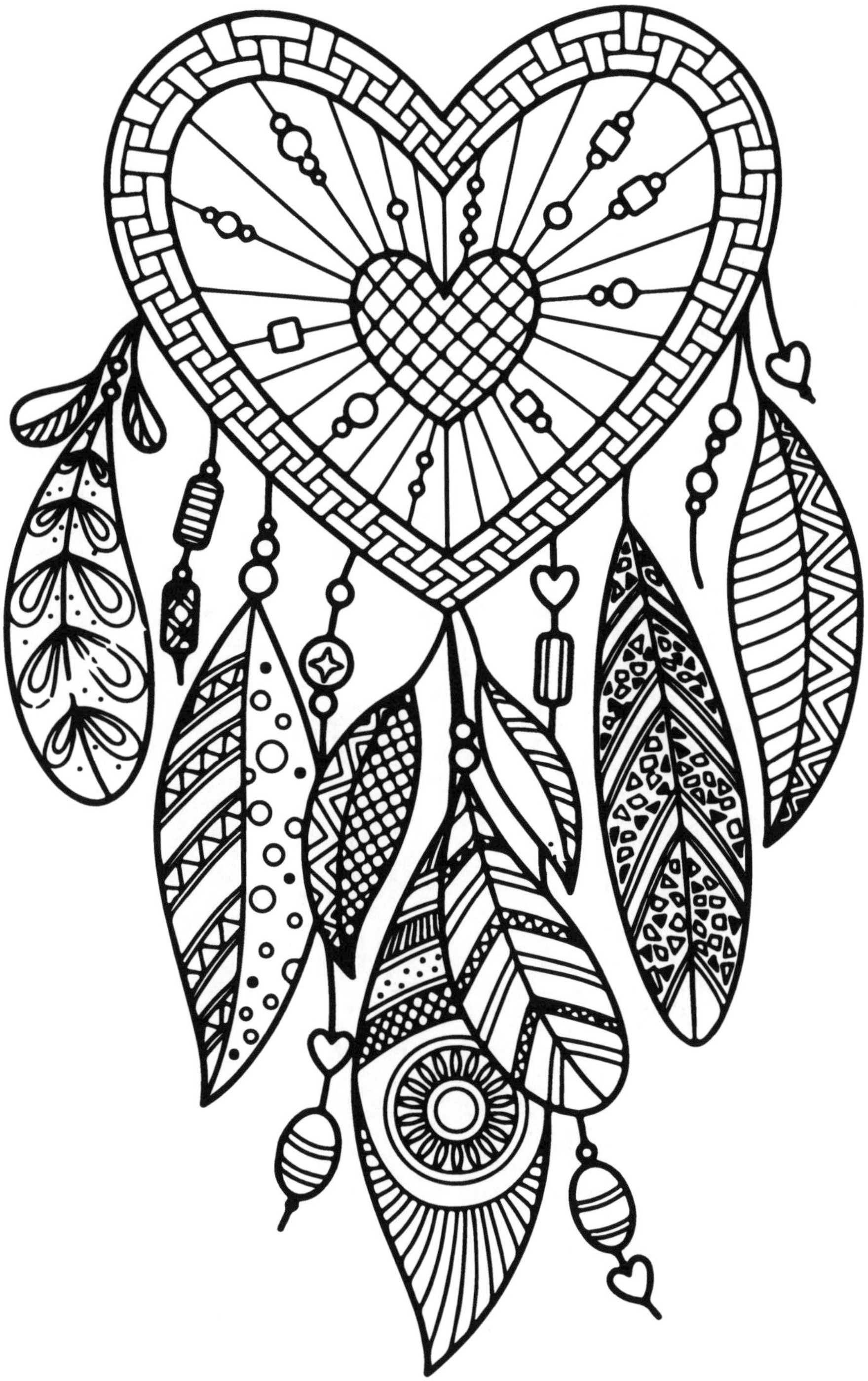

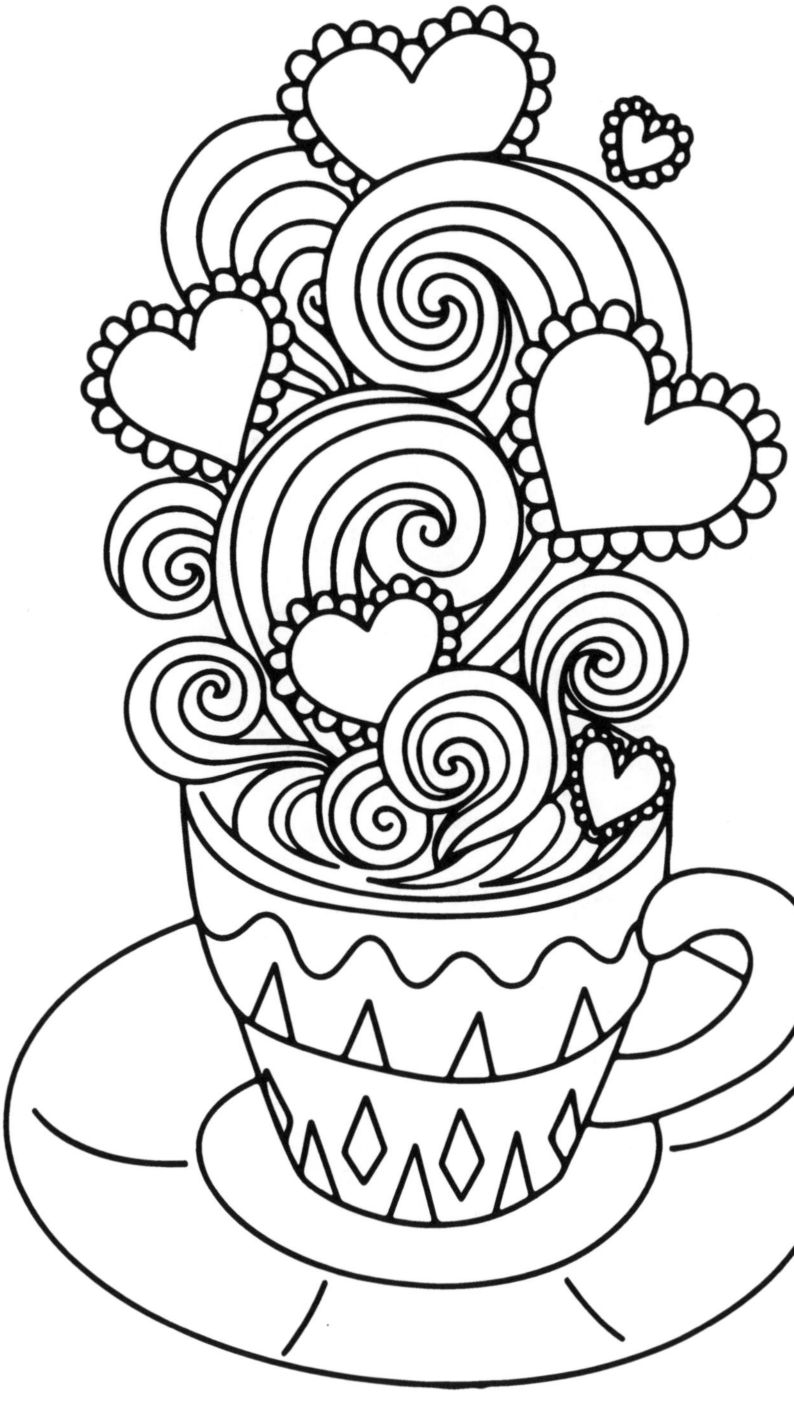

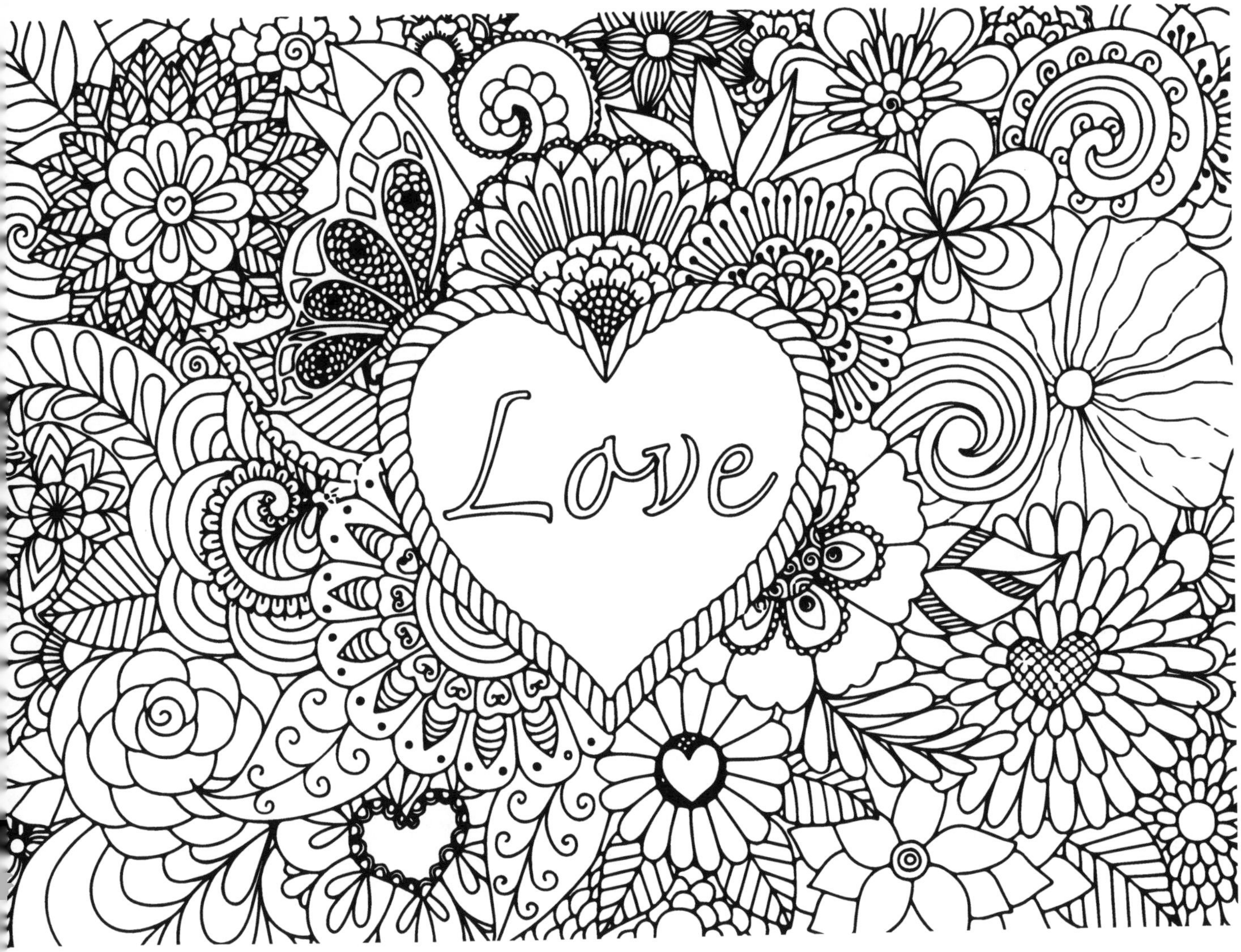
Love

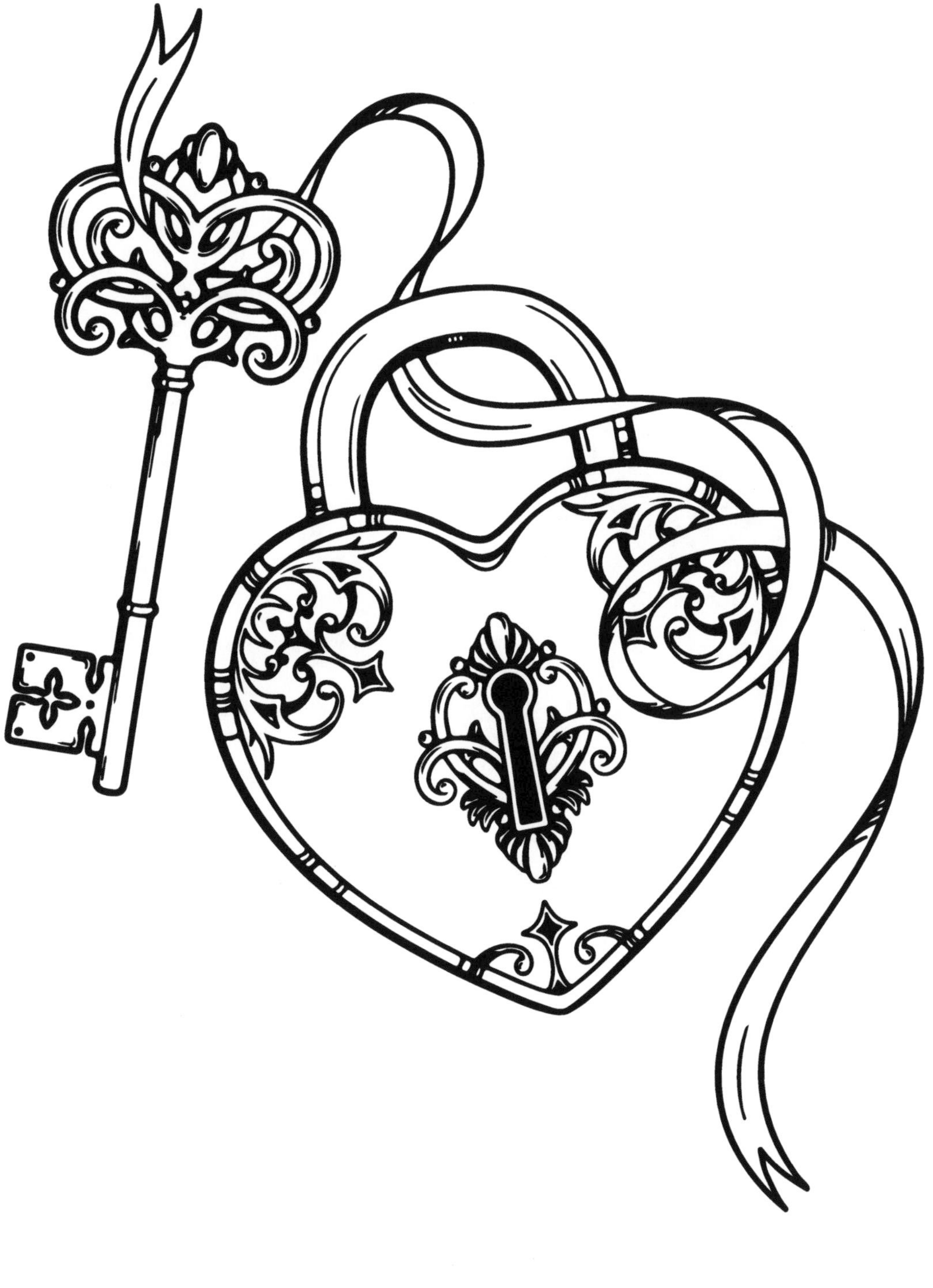

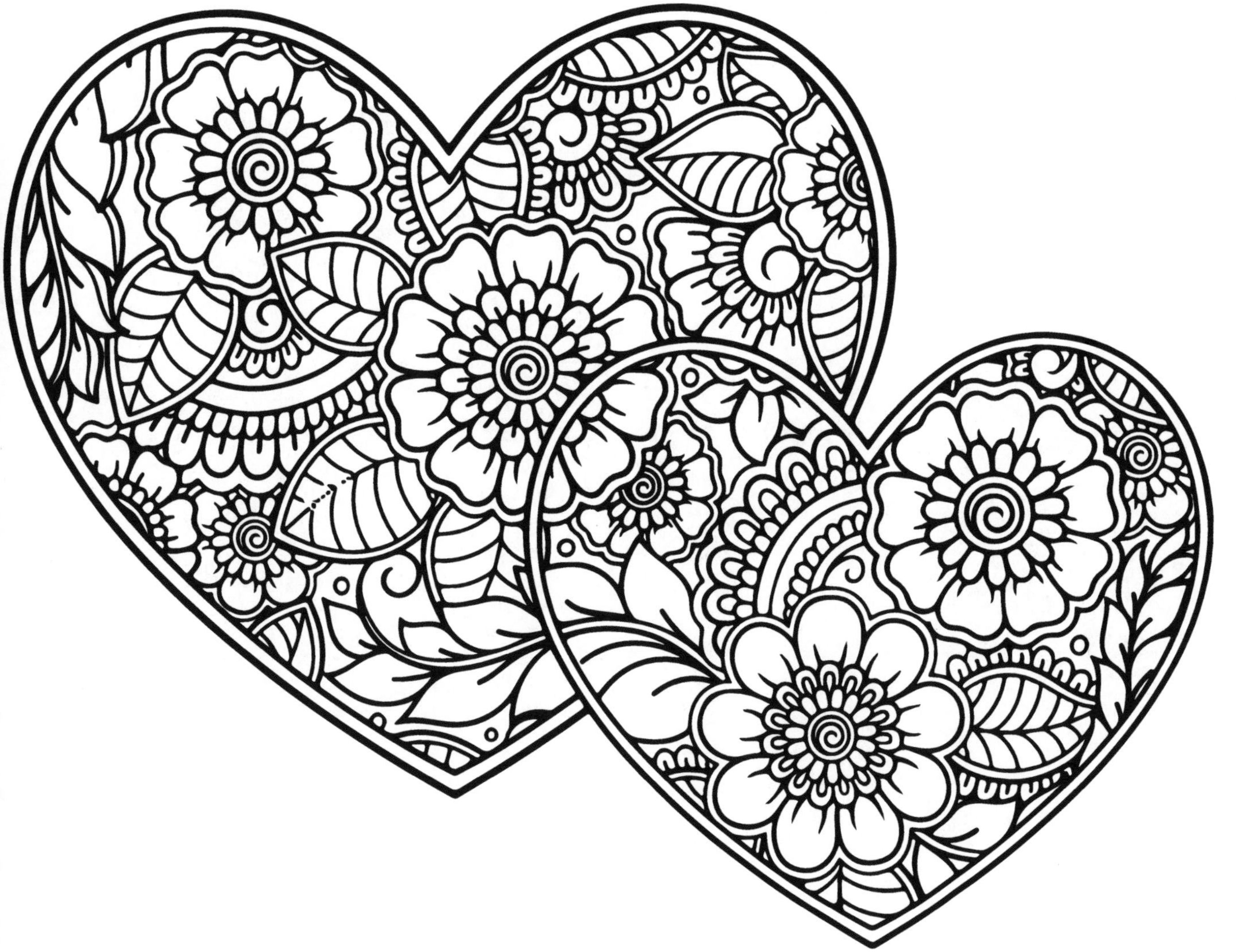

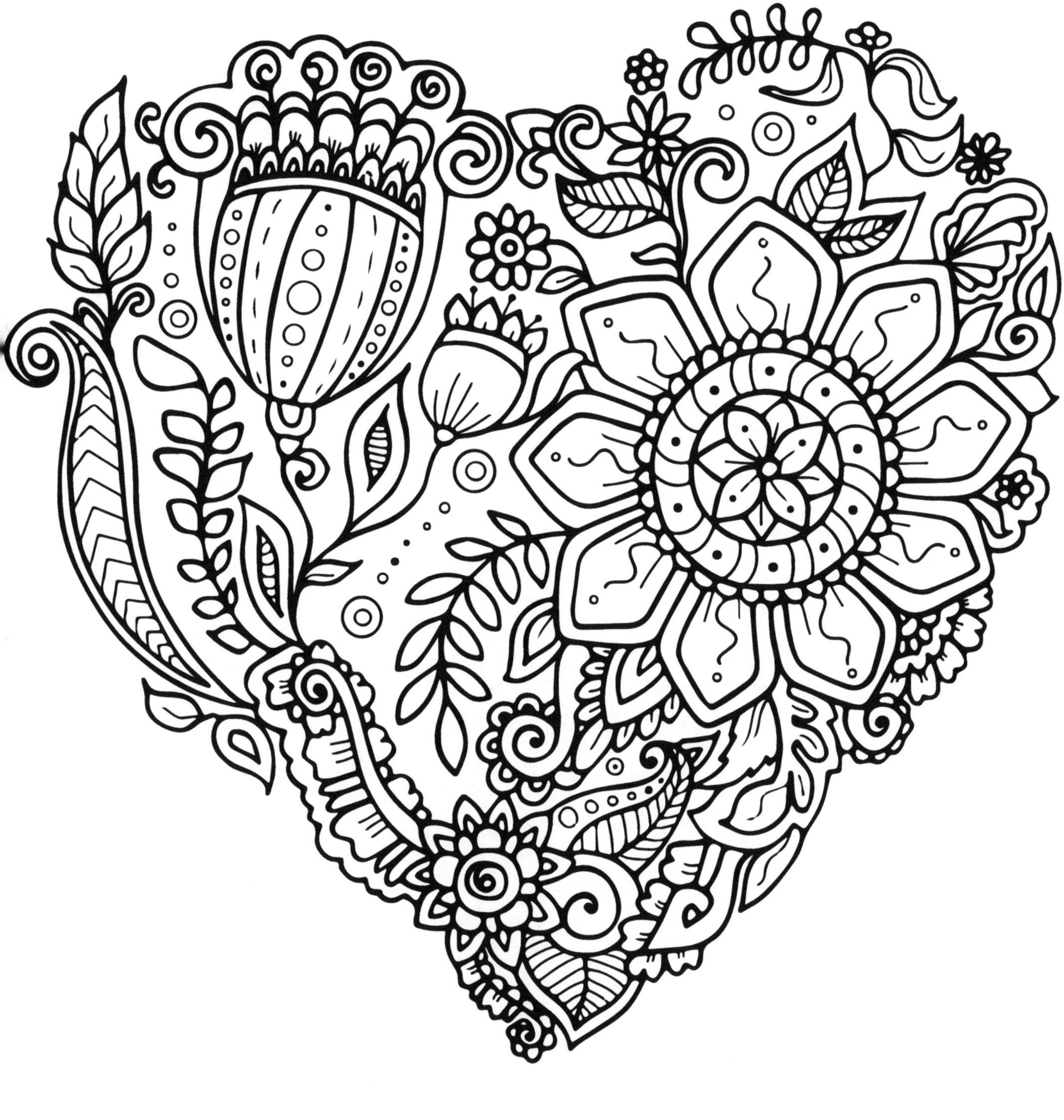

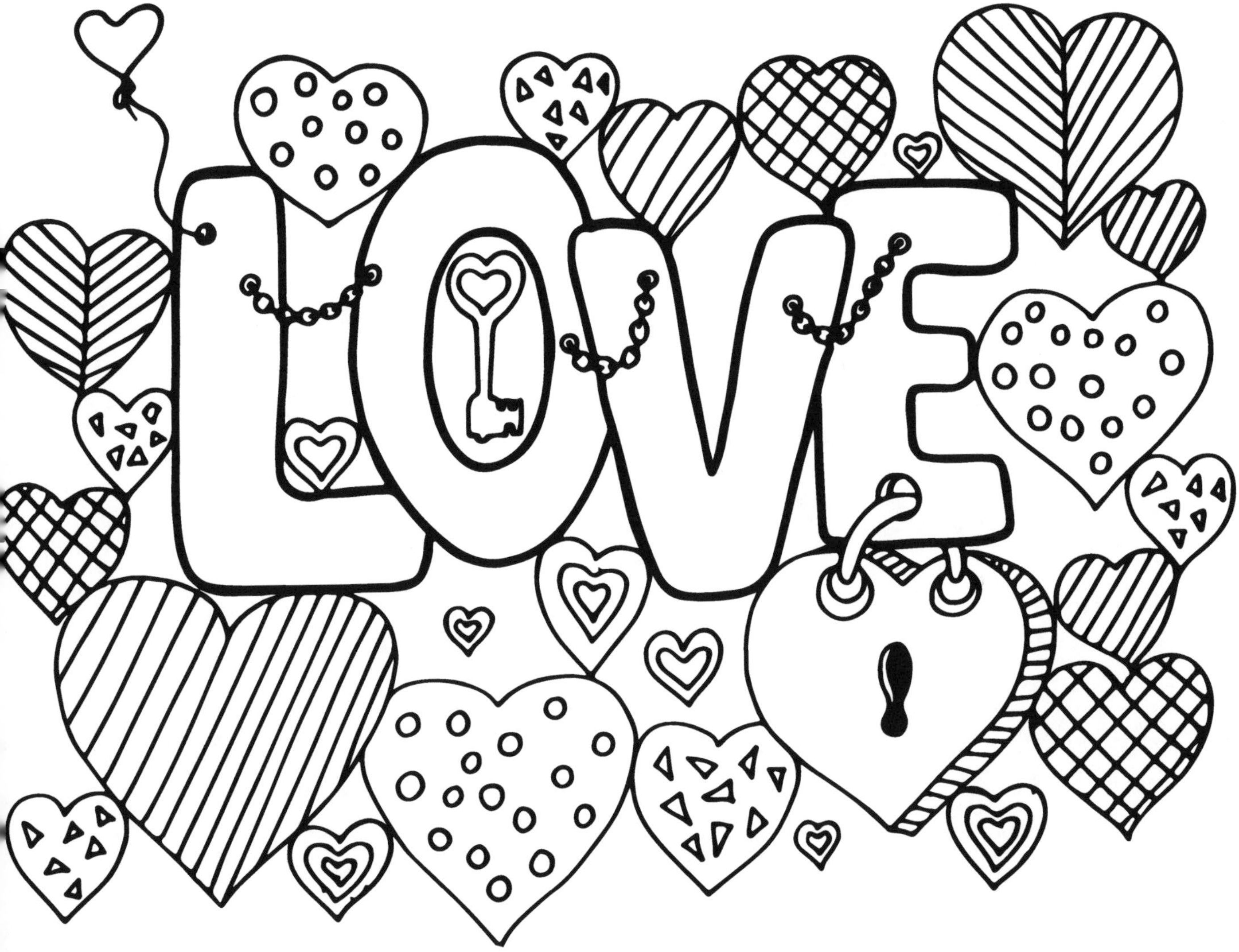
LOVE

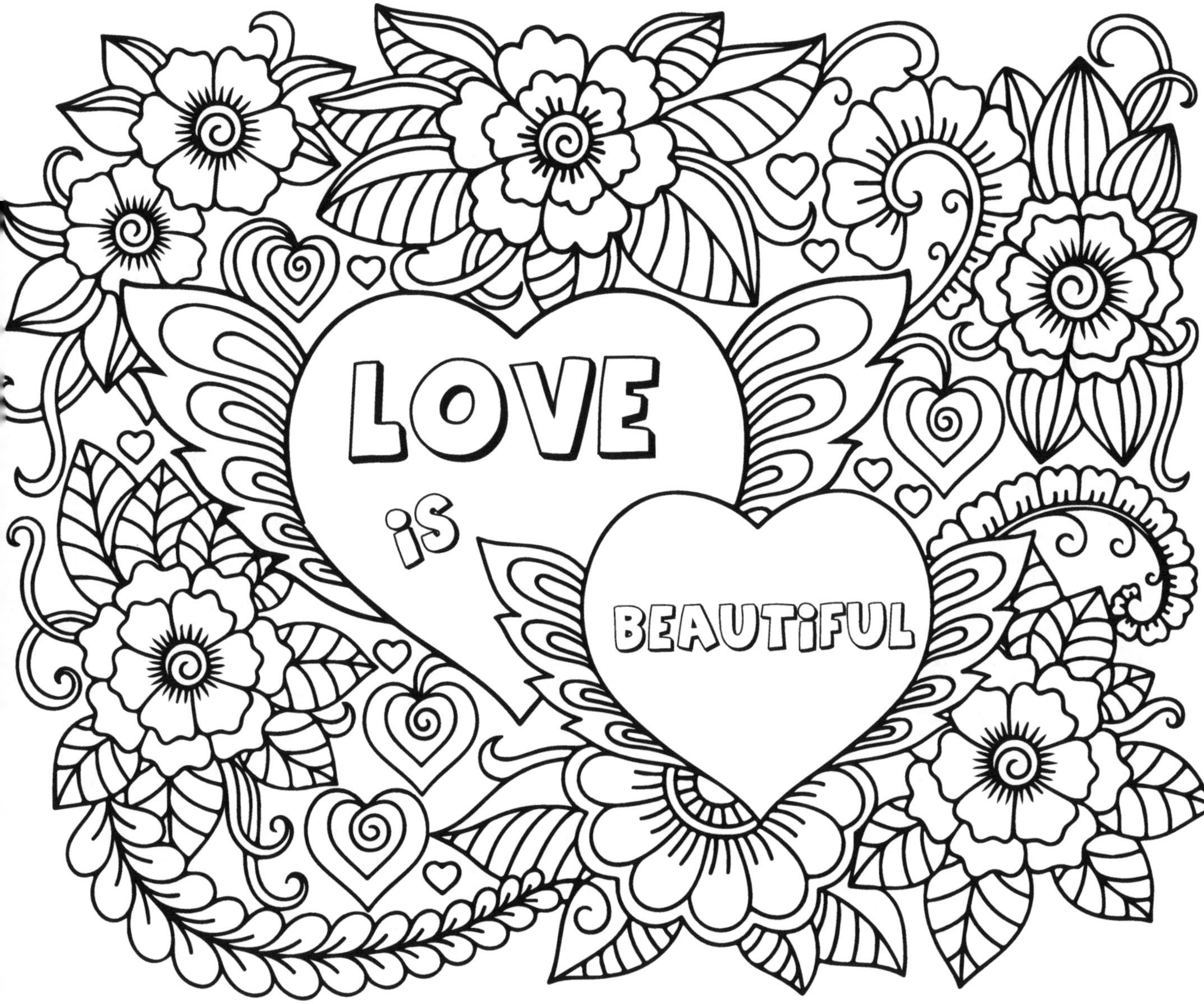
LOVE
iS
BEAUTiFUL

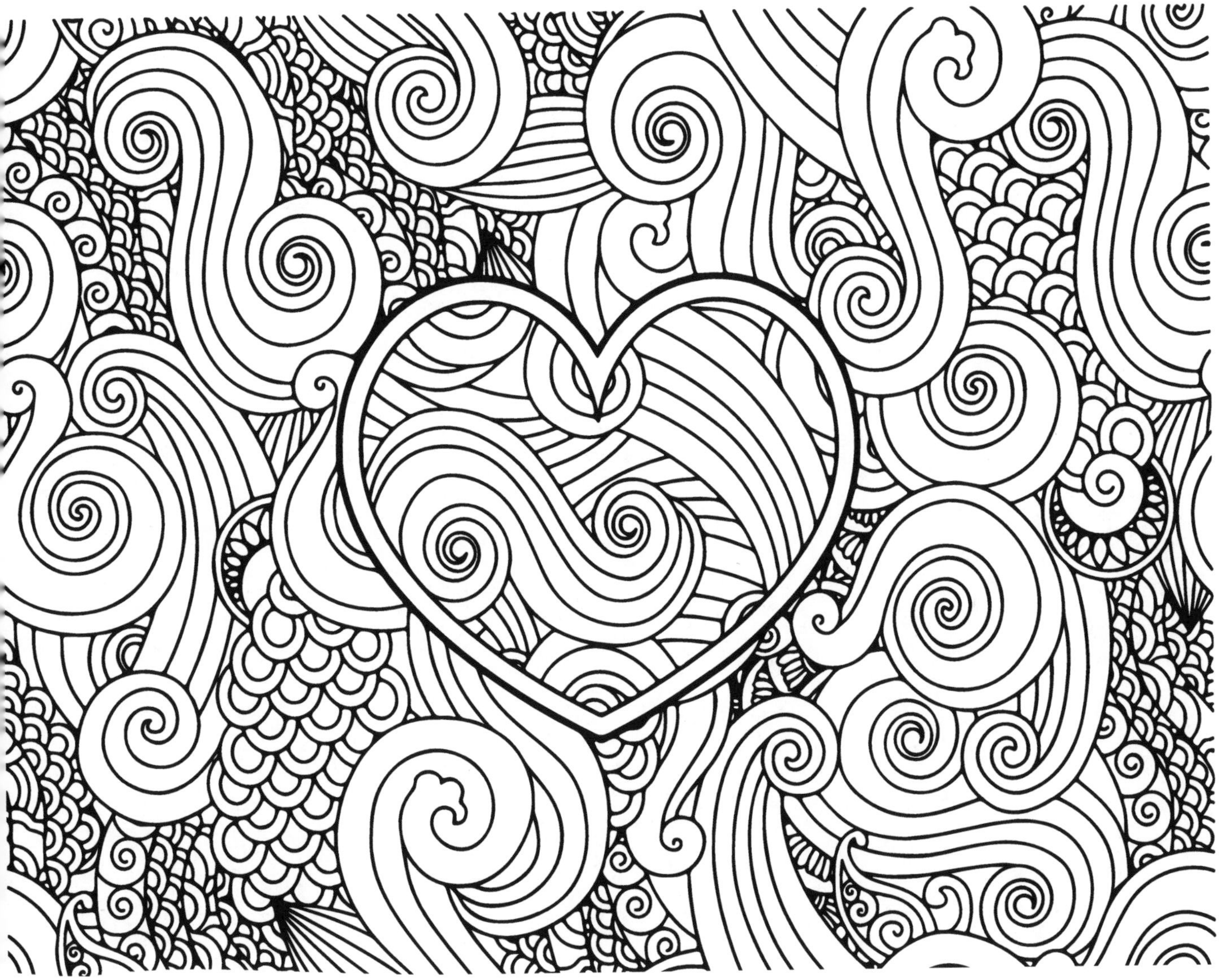

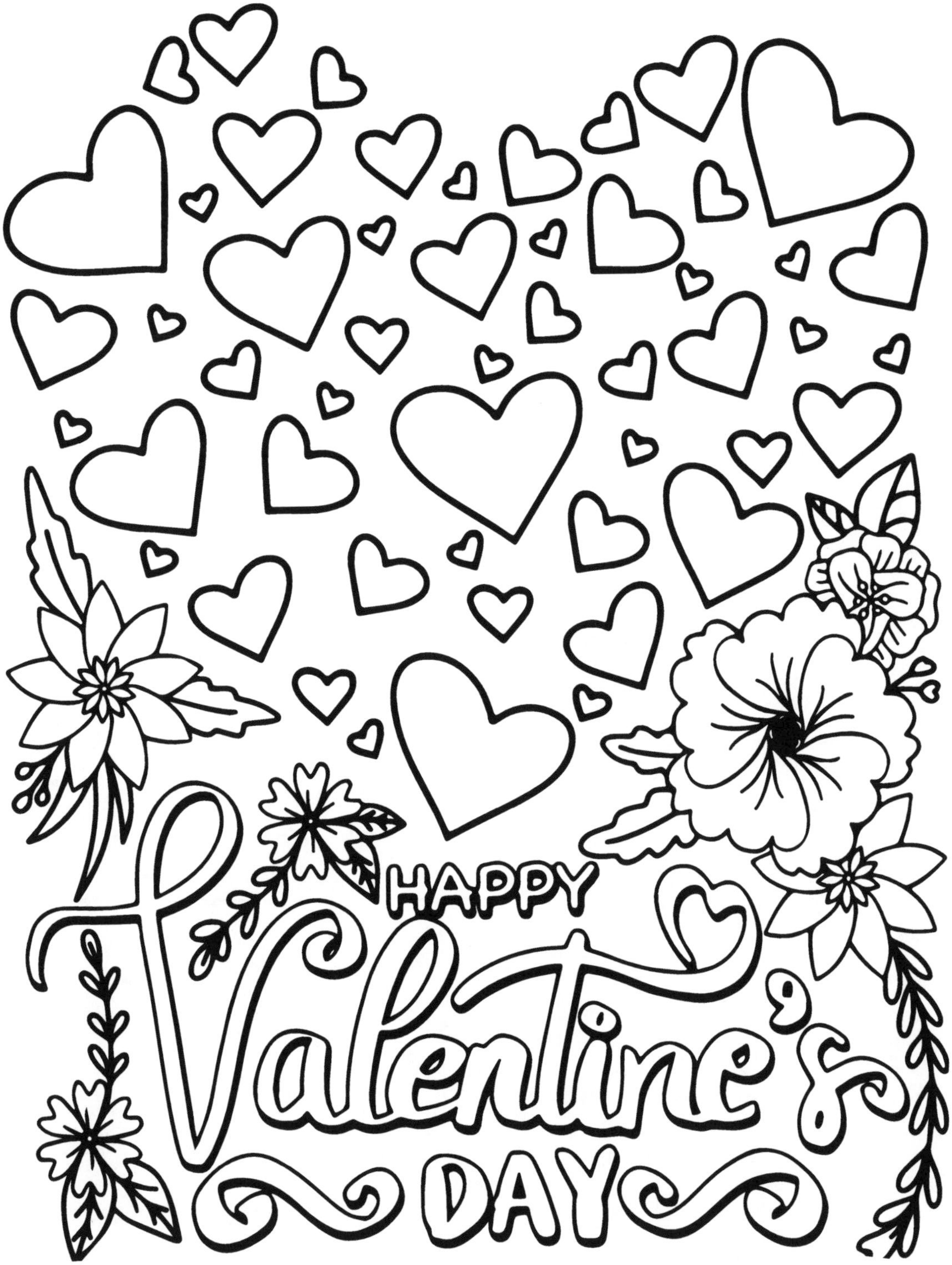
HAPPY
Valentine's
DAY

Made in United States
Orlando, FL
17 February 2023

30067192R00057